TAKE YOUR TIME, GO SLOWLY

After the tragic and sudden death of a child
For the parents and siblings
with no time to say good-bye

by

Ronald Snyder

1663 LIBERTY DRIVE, SUITE 200
BLOOMINGTON, INDIANA 47403
(800) 839-8640
WWW.AUTHORHOUSE.COM

This book is a work of non-fiction. Unless otherwise noted, the author and the publisher make no explicit guarantees as to the accuracy of the information contained in this book and in some cases, names of people and places have been altered to protect their privacy.

© 2005 Ronald Snyder. All Rights Reserved.

No part of this book may be reproduced, stored in a retrieval system, or transmitted by any means without the written permission of the author.

First published by AuthorHouse 03/28/05

ISBN: 1-4208-3734-6 (sc)
ISBN: 1-4208-3775-3 (dj)

Library of Congress Control Number: 2005901918

Printed in the United States of America
Bloomington, Indiana

This book is printed on acid-free paper.

DEFINITIONS OF A CHILD

Webster's Dictionary:

Child; a young human offspring; an infant, boy or girl;

adj.—child's play, a very easy task.

A Parent's Definition:

Child; A part of oneself, body and soul;

Love, joy, pride, welcome challenge.

A wonderful gift from God,

one that truly defies definition.

CONTENTS

Acknowledgments ix

Permissions xiii

Foreword xv

Introduction xvii

Authors Note xix

Chapter One: Grieving 1
    SHOCK 2
    THE NOTIFICATION 4
    FIRST RESPONSIBILITIES AT THE WORST OF TIMES 10
    ACUTE GRIEF 12
    GRIEF 13
    TRIGGERS 15
    OVERVIEW 19

Chapter Two: The Siblings For You, the Brothers and Sisters ... 19
    WHAT THEY SHARE 20
    ON THE ROAD TO HEALING 25

Chapter Three: The Basket of Emotions and the Bag of Tools ... 27
    THE BAG OF TOOLS 30
    BASKET OF EMOTIONS 31

Chapter Four: Emotions 35
    GUILT 36
    SURVIVOR'S GUILT 38
    ANGER 42
    CONDITION RESPONSES 44
    POST-TRAUMATIC STRESS DISORDER 46
    DEPRESSION 46
    SADNESS 51
    ANXIETY 53
    PAIN 55

Chapter Five: Memorials — 57
- A Place and Time 60
- Considering Others 70

Chapter Six: Faith — 75
- Free Will 76
- What God Can't Do 79
- What God Can Do 85
- Christianity 89

Chapter Seven: Other Family Members and Friends — 97
- Loving Relationships 99

Chapter Eight: Healing — 113
- On the Road 114
- Depression-Sadness 115
- Seeking Help 119
- The Healing Powers of Forgiveness 127

Conclusion — 131

Helpful Resources 147

The Compassionate Friends Credo 149

Recommended Reading 151

Sources Cited 153

Acknowledgments

I don't believe a book has ever been written in which an author is immune from the conscious and the subconscious influences we acquire as we travel along life's path. These experiences, good and evil, mold us to some degree. The personalities we develop as we continue to grow cognitively and emotionally will have an impact on ourselves as well as those we will encounter. I am the true beneficiary. Thank you one and all.

First and foremost, I will thank my wife, Sharon. She has always been and continues to be my driving force. My most trustworthy friend and confidant. We have walked the path together, hand in hand, she has always been there to pick me up when I was low and push me when I needed it. Thank you, Sharon, for more than thirty years of faithful encouragement and guidance. Sharon is the love of my life, my compass. With every passing day I love her more; with every passing day I appreciate her more. Her kindness and empathic ways emanate from her to all she encounters, from the days past to today's date. I have always seen this kindness in her heart, and it has been and will always inspire me to be a better person, learning from this woman's example. She is a gift to all that she may encounter. She is a blessing from God.

For my eldest son Brian: All parents welcome their children into this world filled with realistic and unrealistic dreams and expectations. Speaking for your mother as well as myself, let me thank you for that wonderful gift you continually provide. From infancy through childhood, adolescence, and into the adult you have become, you have filled our hearts and souls with the pride and joy that only a parent can truly appreciate. As a son you have fulfilled our dreams and expectations with elation. As a brother and best friend you provided tenderness, love, and compassion. As a parent, you too will write within that book filled with blank pages as you continually experience the rewards and challenges of raising children. As a grandchild, nephew, and cousin you will reap the benefits from those you touch with your heart of gold. If there is one gift I could give you it would not be monetary or those of intrinsic value; it would be the gift of happiness for you to enjoy the rest of your life filled with the many blessings of God.

To my parents Raymond and Betty, thank you both for the many sacrifices as you have always put your children before all others. The snowball effect is evident as you look upon your grandchildren and great-grandchildren. Through your example, you have freely given the tools needed that have enriched our lives forever.

For my parents acquired through marriage, Robert and Shirley, you welcomed me into your wonderful family as you did in your hearts with a single request, that I take good care of your daughter. I hope I have not disappointed you. The both of you are a son-in-law's dream.

To my five brothers and sisters, David, Michael, Donnie, Kim, and Diane, we have survived sibling rivalry at its finest. All of you have blessed my life individually from childhood to date with your kindness and love. You have always supported me and stood by me with comfort. I can only hope I have done the same for you.

The same holds true for my sister-in-law Theresa and brother-in-law Rodney. The both of you are so much like your sister it's uncanny. You have chosen your soul mates wisely, as Rick and Loretta will share the benefit of compassion, love, and trust that I have always recognized as blessings. Thank all of you for the nieces and nephews that continue to thrive in all of our hearts and souls.

As we travel through our lives, we are blessed with the many extended family members and friends that continue to provide support. Some these may not phone on a daily basis, they may not write regularly, but they will be constant reminders of their well wishes and kindness. I would like to thank all such friends, co-workers, and those elsewhere. Especially these I find most dear. The families of Bob S., Brian F., Bob A., Mike P., Greg W., Bob M., Bill and Georgia P., Robbie and Debbie P., Fen and Lynn T., as well as Tony R., Chuck K., Billy and Gail W., Bruce and Tammy, Jimmy H., Ralph B., Ray B., James G., Lonnie B., Bill and Carol H., George and Vicky D., Jackie J. at GSU, and to the best boss I've ever met, Chief Frank Gilbert, who understood the meaning of compassion as he would lead through example where his rules applied to everyone, not just a selected few. This kind man was recognized as the Chief of the Year, awarded in the year 2000 by the South Suburban Chiefs of Police Association. He and his wonderful wife, Sandy, continue to be my friends and will continue to be for years ahead. There are so many others that remain that I could I recall but they are too numerous to mention—you know who you are. Thank You All.

To Deacon Ron at our local parish, you continue to keep in touch with your kind and compassionate ways. Your true reward awaits you.

Thanks will never be enough for the several parishioners at the Northwest Bible Baptist Church located on Bowes Road, unincorporated Kane County. Especially Pastor Dru Deloach and Pedro Nelly, his wife, Mata, and their family.

Last but not least, the entire publishing personnel at Authorhouse who walked me through the delicate progress from start to finish. Amber Olmstead, Robert DeGroff, my Account Managers Josh Clark and Clark Carlson. Without their constant support and encouragement this promise, I fear, would be left unfulfilled.

Permissions

Unless otherwise cited, any correlation between this and any other work shall be considered completely coincidental, academic in nature, and without any foresight intended.

I will, however, take responsibility when recommending further books for my readers for their own benefit without a proper written response to my inquiry.

Thank you.

FOREWORD

Several years ago I attended the funeral for my friend's brother. The minister said something that has remained with me to this day, something I still use in my practice when dealing with grief issues.

In trying to explain the tragic loss of a young man's life, he did not say that it was part to God's plan. Rather, the minister simply stated, "It makes no sense to try and make sense out of things which make no sense," despite our understanding that death is a part of life, a natural consequence of life, and an integral step in the circle of life. To us living, it simply can make no sense. This is especially true when it involves the death of a child, for every child that enters brings into this world his or her own special gift. In every child we see all that is good, all that is promising, all that is innocent, and all that is hopeful. When a beloved child dies, a dream is shattered and a part of each of us dies with them.

More recently I attended the funeral services of a colleague's granddaughter. One of the girl's teachers pleaded to all that "we must do more in our lives. We must do more to make up for this loss, for we must do what she would have done in her lifetime."

This book is about trying to make sense. It is about trying to do more to make up for a loss. In doing so, it echoes the teachings of Terry Cole-Whittaker, a retired television minister and author, who lived and believed that "in life, you must be willing to do whatever it takes to find and become a healthy self." In expressing your courage to be you, you provide others with the courage to be themselves. Ron's courage in writing this book, to reach out to others at the worst time in his life, will inspire those who will read it.

Thomas J. Valente, M.D.

INTRODUCTION

This book is targeted to parents who are suffering after having lost a child due to a catastrophic tragedy. After such a loss, in the beginning our bodies begin a long process and what seems to be a never-ending depression filled with an array of emotions we can't even begin to sort out yet. We feel we are utterly and totally alone. And if it were not for our loved ones and caring friends to help us through, we would be. Even so, some of these kind souls are going to say the wrong things at the wrong time. Things like, "I know how your feeling," or, "It's God's will and someday you'll have all the answers." Such paraphrases are going to cut deep into your soul and hurt so badly you may want to scream, and rightfully so. Know that they are trying to help, they see you're in deep pain, and it hurts them to see you this way. And if they could take your pain and sorrow away they would, but if they have never lost a child in such a way (thank God), in all fairness they don't have a clue. You will find a great need to seek out someone you can relate to, someone who knows the horrible pain you feel, the sickness, the sleepless nights, the uncountable tears streaming down your face as your body shakes and quivers in the shock of it all. Someone who just might understand and help make some sense of it all or, better still, give some of the answers we so desire. Let me say early on, my dear friends, that while we share a heartfelt incurable life event I will not have all your answers, but my promise is that I do understand. I am reaching out to hold your hand and walk with you, and by doing so it is my goal then to in some small way make some reasonable sense of this otherwise twisted world we have recently come only to exist in. We must go on, but only in our own time, and not with someone else's timetable or expectations. You must *Take Your Time, Go Slowly.*

I am not a clergyman, not a psychiatrist, not a clinical psychologist, nor am I a counselor by profession. What I am is a parent. Just like you. Still working his way through the toughest time of my life. Just like you, I still cry. Just like you, my stomach balls in a tight knot every time I reflect upon my son's pictures that are carefully placed about our home, and just like you I continue to search for answers that may never come. But one thing I can say for sure, our lives have changed forever. They will never be the same from that terrible day forward until we are united with our children in heaven.

What I am, however, is a lifelong student of psychology, retired with a career dealing in crisis intervention at every level of life's cycle, but nothing could prepare me for such a loss. I don't think anything can.

During my own and my wife's struggle after our own son's death, it soon became apparent that we had two choices. We were to seek professional help in dealing with our loss or risk, what we thought to be at the time, losing our minds.

Authors Note

As mentioned earlier in the introduction, this book was written for you, the parents and siblings who will continually strive for understanding, being plagued with the many emotions that, if left unchecked and un-dissected, may unnecessarily delay the healthy goal of the healing processes. It is therefore my request that you, the reader, follow the chapters in sequence rather than flip from one to another. These chapters you are about to read were carefully constructed in their design to follow one another; to lead you through the grieving process with the kind and loving care that I believe can be best related from a parent who understands and has experienced the life-changing event after the loss of a child.

Soon after the loss of our second child, my wife and I found ourselves reading anything we could get our hands on relating to the loss of a child. After completing a book we would sit, discuss, and critique the material and its relation to the significance and self-fulfilling qualities that both of us so desperately needed. We longed to speak to a parent who understood what we were facing; this proved to be unsuccessful. I remember speaking with my wife, who agreed that we had yet to discover anything written by an author who had experienced what we were facing. We both agreed that some of the material we were reading was kind and well written; however, we felt unsatisfied with so many matters left unattended.

As she and I faced our frustration, we recognized that what we found available lacked the understanding that only a parent who had lost a child could understand. As for the rest, they did not have a clue. We began searching for support groups with the hope that speaking with others who have walked the path after their loss might lead us to a better understanding of the devastation that had returned to us from twenty-seven years earlier. Revisiting acute grief led us to a crisis with our faith. We felt angry with God and the world in general. I proposed that something should be written in the context of a personal nature from someone who could truly relate to others who might have found themselves in this situation. It was shortly after that I began to write this book with the hope and strong desire that it be received well and that it might help others who might otherwise remain in turmoil.

Let us attempt to come to some reasonable understanding by sorting and dissecting these emotions that we have come to understand as despair and depression. May God bless us, help us, and walk with us as we embark upon this road less traveled, together, hand in hand, from the notification to the promise of a better self, a healthier self within the final chapter on healing.

ಸ CHAPTER ONE ಚ

GRIEVING

Before we begin, let us remind ourselves that we are all aware of the fact that "we will never know where we're going unless we know where we've been; lest history shall repeat itself." This history lesson is important for those of us facing the lifelong road ahead. We need to understand that many of us are cognitively aware of the challenges we have come to face and it can often be beneficial to have the many emotions explained and dissected for us by someone who understands and can relate to others having faced the worst fear on earth, losing a child.

Some of what you're about to read within chapters one and two may be uncomfortable depending on your own place in time physically, mentally, and spiritually. It is with the strongest desire and a promise that after doing so you will come to a better, healthier understanding, just knowing we are not alone in our newfound world as our lives have changed today and forever more.

SHOCK

The mind and body manifest themselves to a place they seldom go. You are numb, totally overcome with extreme sadness; you may feel as if your very life is being drained from your body onto the floor and you're helpless to recover. For initial shock, the physical effects become all too real. You feel as if your heart is about to pound through your chest, your head is about to explode. Temporally immobilized as you're emotions begin to set in, you are completely overcome.

My friends, you have just begun a lifelong journey filled with many emotions that need to be sorted out. As I have mentioned earlier, it is my goal to help you and yours sift through this newly discovered BASKET OF EMOTIONS that has been dropped in your lap at the worst time in your life. With the BAG OF TOOLS, together we will sort, organize, and design a workable game plan of dissection that in time will bring some sanity back into your life again. Rest assured you are not on a collision course with the nut house, and even if you believe you're well on your way to the funny farm, keep in mind you're experiencing emotions of such great magnitude you may need a helping hand to ease your way. The alternative most likely will be prolonged, or what's better referred to as extended, grief that is unnecessary.

Grieving

Grief after losing a child will be unlike any other emotion you will ever be faced with. You might feel as if you're alone—oh my, friends, let me assure you that you're not. The forthcoming stories that others were willing to share, for your sake as well as their own, were given with permission to be passed on to you freely. With kindness in their hearts, they hoped their experiences would help someone else find the way on this path we must all walk, however slowly, to reach the goal of returning to one's true self, knowing our lives have changed forever.

Before we move from shock into acute grief, just before grieving, you will discover a newfound set of priorities. What seemed to be important matters in the past are now trivial. Your life will have new meaning, a new course of direction, with a new set of rules and guidelines to travel. The journey is long and difficult but rest assured, my friends, from a father who has lost two children, I share your grief. In our own timetable, we will together walk the path, stumble and fall, and pick ourselves up again and again, and continue walking along the way on this treacherous path, knowing we will make it. We have to: there are too many other people depending on us. We may have to put some things on hold, but as we have done with our recently discovered new priorities so realignment of responsibilities cannot be ignored. First and foremost should be to take care of yourself.

By neglecting your own needs right now you will not be in any shape to care for loved ones who so desperately need you. At this time you may feel you're lacking the energy, motivation, or simply the desire to be there, but remember that we all have our own timetable. For each of us it will be different; don't allow others to impose their beliefs on you. Your path has many twist and turns, much different than others around you, and each and every one of you must respect each other's needs; give them the room and with a watchful eye give comfort whenever possible as the loving caring person you are. Looking outside yourself you'll soon rediscover that what has only been on hold for a short time awaits your guidance. You'll find it again in the eyes of your remaining children, your grandchildren. The siblings may be young or may be mature, adult brothers or sisters; whatever the case, they need your attention and comfort as much as you need theirs. Don't forget that they, a father, mother, brother, or sister, cry, hurt, and they too have discovered the basket of emotions as you did. As you continue to read on, you will find some things that will ring true. Consider them gifts to share with your loved ones, a tool to place in your bag of tools explained later in chapter three.

THE NOTIFICATION

Notification comes to us in many ways, none of which will be acceptable. For some it may be a knock on the door just when, moments before you, were enjoying a relaxing evening with your husband or wife. Dinner past, dishes cleaned and put away, you're kicking back reading or simply enjoying a program on television.

Grieving

You don't have a clue that the knock on the door is about to change your life forever. Answering the door, you're greeted by a police officer who asks to come in. He states he has to speak to you about something that has happened. Your instincts begin to kick in, you become alarmed, and you feel an uncontrollable trembling through your body. You know something's wrong—bad wrong.

Opening the door wider, you invite him in. If he's a professional and has experience in the horrible task of the notification, he will begin by introducing himself and asking you to sit down and ask permission to sit himself. He should choose a chair facing you directly, knowing your undivided attention would soon be at hand. Compassionately, this officer will look you in the eye and begin to explain that a tragic event has recently taken place and ask if he can call a friend or family member to the home to help you with what he's about to discuss. Now you're beginning to panic; one of the strongest emotions becomes evident (fear). To the officer who realizes his task can't wait any longer, with or without a support person the officer, if he's worth his weight, will not dance around the matter at hand. He will kindly and sincerely unfold the current events informing you your son or daughter has been involved in a tragic accident that has clamed his or her life. The officer will tell you the details pertinent for the notification, leaving the minute details for a later date. The experienced officer will remain with you to answer any and all questions, however difficult, knowing you need the truth, and remain in room the with you as long as it takes to offer the advice that only a professional can give.

Unfortunately, not all police officers are created equal. Know that there are those out there that are callous at best, without the social skills needed to be a police officer, all too many of whom fall through the cracks. They pass sophisticated screenings and are cut loose upon an unknowing community at their mercy with the misconception that these officers are of the proper caliber to serve and protect and do it well. For those of you who have faced an unkind, uneducated officer this will only add to your grief, now and forever. Personally I am ashamed for such officers and can only apologize for their lack of empathy, and I assure you that the officers under my supervision were never sent on a notification without my full confidence that they obtained the skills and compassion to aid and not traumatize such a delicate responsibility. If I had any doubts, I would always make the time to handle this myself. I know this can be of little consolation after the damage has been done. Of all the ways and reasons to receive the notification after the tragic death of a child, the most common will be that of a police officer.

No matter what the cause of death, whether it is an automobile accident, drug overdose, murder, or suicide, the notification, as I've mentioned, will always be followed by shock. Your parish priest, your closest family member, friend, or neighbor—it's all the same: confusion, distress, disbelief, and complete denial. I share these thoughts with you, not to hurt you but to help make you aware that your emotions are shared by all of us who can relate like no other can. All the reasoning and theorizing in the world cannot hold a hand out to you to comfort you and walk with you without having experienced such a loss. That's not to say there is no good literature out there to help. Quite the contrary; there are some wonderful things on the shelves these days, and later I will recommend some of them for you. But be aware that as there are unskilled police officers so there are unskilled authors. Be selective; get references. You may not be able to choose the means by which you receive the notification but you can wisely choose a therapist, doctor, or even a good book by asking the right questions. We'll speak more about that later.

Allow me to share my notification. For some, your experience has been similar. My wife and I settled in for the evening after treating ourselves to a night out for dinner. Two hours earlier I had a phone conversation with my youngest son, twenty-four years of age. During this conversation he expressed with great excitement that the day had finally arrived. He was so excited he was giddy. He was moving down from Chicago to Florida to join us, his truck packed and ready for the long-awaited trip, and it was eminent.

"I can't wait, Dad. I'm on my way. I can't wait. I love you so much, I can't tell you how much. I promise, Dad, and don't you worry; if I get tired on my way I'll pull over, call you, and get some sleep. I can't promise that I'll sleep a lot, because I know I'll be excited and I'll want to start driving again. I don't care if I get tired, I'll just stop again and get some more rest until I wake. I'll get something to eat and start on my way again. I'm on my way. I'll be there soon. I just can't wait. I'll see you and Mom soon."

I told him how much I loved him and made him promise again for my own reassurance that he would be careful and arrive safely, and he stated, "Okay, Dad, I promise. Please don't worry, and tell Mom not to worry either. I do love you both. Soon I'm on the way."

I discussed the phone conversation with Sharon during dinner and she complained how she wished she had not gone shopping so she could have spoken with him. They had a relationship second to none; they were buddies. After the dinner, as I mentioned we relaxed a while and went to bed. We were resting well when the phone rang. It was about 11:15 p.m. I nudged Sharon to get the phone that was placed on her side of the bed on the nightstand. I heard her answer, "Okay. Ron? Sure, he's right here." Sharon drifted back into sleep as I answered. It was my brother David on the phone.

"Ron? Are you there?"

"Yes, Dave, what's up?" I could sense something was wrong, as if he might have been crying. He continued.

"I've been trying to reach you for a while but there was no answer, so I kept calling, waiting for you to pick up. Ron, I need you to wake up. I have to talk to you."

"Okay, Dave, I'm awake. What is it?"

"I'm so sorry, brother, to give news like this." He started crying and I felt myself going numb.

"Dave, it's okay. Dave, what has happened?"

I did not have a clue what was about to happen. David said, "It's your son, he's been ... he's been in a terrible accident, Ron. God, I wish I were there with you." His crying became more intense.

"David, what has happened?" I repeated. "David...."

"I don't know how to tell you."

"Dave, there's only one way and you know it, don't you?" Looking at Sharon, I checked. *Good, she's still sleeping.* "Dave, just tell me, did he survive? Is he dead, Dave?" And I'll never forget his next words, all too simple, all too plain in consideration. David said the one thing that every parent has the worst nightmares about, the kind that wake you from a restful sleep to total uncontrolled panic.

David finally brought himself to say, "I'm so sorry, brother, your son is dead, and he did not ... he didn't make it." For those of us who have received this type of notification, the rest of what follows is no different from those mentioned previously. Shock. God help us all.

For some, shock will last for days, for others it will last for weeks. Remember that each of us has our own timetable through the stages of grief. It will seem as if we can't go on. We make ever so small, tiny steps forward only to encounter a trigger that will send us back into despair. It's so important that we all must rely on our family, hopeful that they will recognize the symptoms in each other that may require intervention. Don't be fearful to step forward and voice your concerns if you see something that seems important, something that may need to be addressed by a professional. It will always be better to play it safe than allow a loved one to suffer needlessly.

In the confusion and turmoil of shock, we are confronted with responsibilities that require our attention without delay. Some of these things you must handle yourself, but there are others to be delegated as we continue to move on and travel this winding path.

FIRST RESPONSIBILITIES AT THE WORST OF TIMES

Still in a state of shock, you may feel depleted of energy. We are faced with some essential decisions that require our imminent attention at an all-time low in our lives. You're feeling the effects of shock; you're sick to your stomach, so sick the very thought of eating brings you to the point of nausea, and well-intentioned family keep pushing food in front of you. Police and the media confront you to answer questions, well-wishers telephoning. We would like to run and hide, but we can't. There are the funeral arrangements to make and music to decide on for the church. There may be a memorial service, and who will speak? Who was your child's favorite priest or pastor? What flowers will be appropriate? Have all of your child's friends been notified? Everyone will have questions. There will be neighbors knocking at your door with well wishes, and they'll want to see you to express their condolences. All these require your attention, and all you can do to survive this event of your life is to muster enough strength to get from one room to another, keeping a watchful eye on what remains of your fragmented family.

Grieving

Your plate is full, my friends, and you don't need it complicated any further. For some, you may be facing a visit to the coroner's office at their request to make a final identification. This can be as traumatic as the notification. Your cup runneth over. Please take my advice. Yes, there are many things you must attend to, but some things can be delegated to a family member or a close friend. Your spouse and children, your grandchildren need you: all of you need to be together. Free yourself of some of the demands of others. Take your responsibilities one at a time. Everything you have to do cannot and will not be done in the next ten minutes. You're not going to remember every little detail. You're on overload, and the comfort of knowing that a trusted member of your extended family or a close friend is there keeping an eye on you and your wants and wishes will free you and your mind, making it easier to handle the most important tasks that demand your personal attention and allow others to help. You will find them eager to do whatever they can.

Consider how helpless they feel and how they would welcome any opportunity in any small way to rush to your aid, answering the telephone, taking messages, or releasing what information you have gone over with them. Knowing that information of a personal nature will be respected is very important, so before delegating it will require just a few minutes of direction. For example, if a wake is planned your delegate can free you up by standing at the entrance to help with any introductions. When I mentioned you being on overload I was stating a scientific fact. The human brain is only capable of processing a given amount of information at one time. With the event at hand, and the fact that you're most likely still in shock or at the very least acute grief (the next stage of the mourning cycle), your mind is overloaded and you're far from being yourself. This helpful delegate can politely attend to such things without your being uncomfortable.

After the funeral or memorial service, you return home and maybe for the first time as you walk past your child's bedroom, your denial may begin to take on a different perspective. Your denial could still come and go, fading ever so slightly. As the reality of your loss becomes more and more evident, so too comes the reality of that basket of emotions you and your family may soon find yourself engulfed in—acute grief.

ACUTE GRIEF

A father writes, soon after the tragic and sudden death of his twenty-four-year-old son, struck down in an accident by a young nineteen-year-old driver on a rainy evening on the west side of Chicago:

> *"What is this place we have come to know as the dark, dark hole filled with uncontrollable tears, extreme sadness, sickness mental and physical? This place I speak of must be hell on earth, for I can find no other reasonable explanation."*

Acute grief immediately follows shock. For those of us in it we know all to well the shallowness, the loneliness, and the debilitating sadness here is very much like the shock we have recently left behind. Acute grief in its most serious condition can best be described as Post-Traumatic Stress Disorder (PTSD), a conduction that follows a traumatic life event clinically diagnosed from a large range of symptoms that expanded beyond that of depression. There are many qualifying indicators of PTSD, and, as with any prolonged or alarming indicator, let us please not delay. Get your loved ones to a professional where help and a healthy recovery is very near. This is not to imply that acute grief will not run its normal course; it is only brought to your attention for you to recognize and become aware of the fact that not all of us will progress as well as we would like. If we can, we should alleviate any undue pain for our loved one. Let's waste no time.

GRIEF

At a time when you are at that in-between point of acute grief and grief, you may feel the basket of emotions consuming you, threatening your very existence. For many of us, and those I have spoken with personally, we describe our physical being as that of not being whole. We see ourselves as a shell of what we once were, hollow and drained of resources. We feel out of place without our child or sibling. Thoughts of suicide fade in and out of the conscious mind. What is most desired is to hold the child just one more time, one more kiss.

From a mother to her son: Oh my son, I try to remember all the good times you gave me, the love, the warmth of your wonderful smile. How you would pick me up from home and we would walk around the mall holding hands as you smiled with joy and pride.

The mall inundated with your former classmates, you felt no embarrassment. You spoke of how we need to get away like this more often. You never complained, only stared at me and smiled. The love we share will be ever lasting. When I go for walks and feel the warm breeze rushing through my hair, the bright sunlight upon me, I feel your hand. Your presence is with me. I imagine you glancing down upon me with the smile that brings such pleasure to my soul. Know that I do not fear death anymore; rather, I welcome it, and in good time, my son, we will walk that mall again. I love you, I miss you so.

It would appear this mother is well on her way to a healthy self. I would not make the mistake of assuming that this mother is free of turmoil. Just as all of us, she will suffer the pains of her loss her entire life. She too will have triggers that will overcome her with such intensity only a mother can know.

Triggers

The triggers we will encounter along our life's journey will be abundant. They will come upon us in many different ways. Some of these triggers will be welcome distractions filled with love and joy, while others will rock our world and temporarily send us back into extreme sadness.

In the beginning, soon after the loss of a child, anything and everything will hold some significant value during acute grief. The friends our child knew, played with, or, given the opportunity, grew up with often become extended family members themselves. Now, soon after our loss, we discover the effect our child has had on others who will come to you in their own shock asking all kinds of questions, and they will need the answers. They will want to share with you the good old days that we have all come to realize were the days taken for granted. You will look upon these young people with a new fear, and you find yourself asking them or telling them to take care of themselves with new meaning.

I remember my wife and I one evening as we sat next to one another, a silence was broken as we began talking about these other children who recently left our company overcome with disbelief and sadness. We spoke about our joined fears and prayed they be spared such a fate that had taken our son. We feared for their lives. All parents' greatest fear of losing a child had become a reality for us, and we prayed that the families of our extended ones would not suffer in the world we now only exist in. Let these others be more understanding of the fact that the life they have is not to be taken for granted, but cherished and used well. Let them mature with the promise of a life filled with dreams that come true and the opportunity to appreciate them, every one. I will mention that friends are not to be taken for granted, and so it was true for my son's closest—you know who you are. Thank you, Phil, Matt V., Matt Vs., Rich, Troy, Carl Jeanna, and Robin. This writer, like you, will not be spared the triggers that will send us from one place to another, like that of a stone sent soaring into the air by some slingshot without direction to land where it may. Each and every one of the above friends I've mentioned here is a joyful and comforting reminder of our son. If I could give them any gift it would have to be the gift of gratitude for being such an important part of my son's life.

    The months will pass, as will the years, and as they do you will develop coping skills that will ease your way, but not without some sadness and hopefully, with time, some joy.

    Be prepared, my friends, that as the good and joyful memories of our children replace those of anger and fear (explained in chapter four) you will not be spared the occasional slingshot into the past due to one of the many triggers we will encounter throughout our lives.

    As this book was written for those parents and siblings who have lost children due to a tragedy and sudden death, we cannot ignore the fact that we will encounter other parents along the way who suffer and grieve as we do. It is for this reason I have chosen a few stories with the permission of the parents, to share in an effort to help make you aware that while losing a child tragically and suddenly is still in the minority in this country, childhood deaths with some warning or preparation will never be easy for the parents. Quite the contrary, they will feel the pain and the triggers that will send them on that journey we will share. The loss of a child holds no boundaries. We will study family members and how our loss is their loss, just to a lesser degree, in chapter seven.

Triggers can and will approach us when we least expect it. One moment we may be relaxing, engulfed in some program on television, and it will come without warning or reason, as if someone just slapped your face. You may find yourself choked up, fighting tears. Some trigger has sent you back in time with no rhyme or explanation; it's just there. You may be driving to the grocery store and on the radio will come a piece of music that will remind you of your child; in some cases a sense of joy will overcome you, while at other times the same piece of music can bring you to sadness.

We may find ourselves walking in a shopping mall, and overhear a child calling out, "Mom, watch this!" or, "Hey Dad, wait up!" The voice will have an uncanny resemblance to the voice of the child we have lost. We may find ourselves frozen in time. Others pass us by while we feel our hearts pounding, our faces turning flush. We hesitate to turn, to locate this voice from the past, knowing disappointment will soon be upon us. Nevertheless, we turn and after locating the source, we will be saddened to tears. An embarrassing moment to say the least, but it is just as uncontrollable as our desire, a temporary lapse from realty. You will find the delusion obtrusive.

Other triggers may include news broadcasts of tragic events involving children completely unknown just minutes before. This will remind you of the first days that followed your life-changing event, and your heart will go out to the parents and families, whom we know have only just begun the journey we know all too well. We will without doubt have a strong desire to reach out to help the families on their way; on their path less traveled.

There are as many triggers as there are parents, siblings, and other family members that will be unique to them alone, and other triggers that will be shared with family and strangers alike. Of this I know: all will encounter the moments consciously and subconsciously. I hope and pray that as time heals and the nights fade from unhappy dreams of our loved ones, that they are replaced with ones that bring you and yours peace and happy memories filled with the joy that will serve as true reminders of the gift that will be with us all forever, in our hearts, minds, and souls. All we need to do is remind ourselves and those around us as we find the need. This will be especially true for the siblings.

Take your time, go slowly.

ॐ CHAPTER TWO ॐ

THE SIBLINGS FOR YOU,
THE BROTHERS AND SISTERS

Overview

As children grow, they develop a bond that is unique to them alone. They learn early in life and into adulthood, that what they share is to be held in the highest regard. Often siblings will enter into a personal pack in which they go to great lengths to protect. They, like so many close friends, may go so far as to swear to the ultimate commitment of trust. Their childlike behavior directs them to cross their hearts, spit in the air, and seal their lips forevermore or suffer as only a traitor may suffer. As an adult this brings back many memories of our own childhood and the fresh recollection of such an intense promise to one another. However insignificant and humorous it may be to us now, we can't help but remember how important it was during those days filled with the trust of a brother or sister. After all, not all things were to be shared with the parents, right?

What They Share

A brother told me a story about when he and his brother Corey were being grounded to a downstairs room and were not allowed to go outside and play for a while. He and his younger brother by four years concocted a daring game:

"If caught we knew our actions would be met with the greatest of repercussions, but the excitement of the deceitful game against our parents, sitting just upstairs, was our way of rebelling. And yet in another way, it was just a way for the two of us at the age of about ten and six to carry out a daring feat of courage, and success was our reward. We were to take turns sneaking up the ten or so flights of stairs ever so quietly, undetected, stick our tongues out at Mom and Dad, then return again so quickly to the awaiting brother. We would laugh at this great accomplishment, patting each other on the back. 'We did it, we really did it! Man, that was great,' we would say. One after the other we would take turns, time and time again, until one time one of us got caught and we both received an added sentence of fifteen minutes to the grounding. It wasn't as bad as we thought it would be, maybe even a little disappointing, for the risk seemed, at the time at least, to outweigh the deed. Well, if we hadn't laughed hard enough before, after listening to Mom and Dad upstairs discussing our initiative and breaking out in laughter themselves at the thought of it, we looked at each other confused and we came to realize the game had played full circle. There we were downstairs and the more we laughed, the more Mom and Dad laughed."

We have to remember that our children do not share everything with us (the parents) but they do confide in their brothers and sisters. As mentioned earlier, brothers and sisters will share their innermost feelings, and after the loss of a sibling, they will soon discover they have lost their most trusted confidant in their world; their best friend is lost forever. They feel they have lost a witness of their own life.

Families have become smaller throughout the years, and for siblings with only one brother or sister they may feel like the only survivor after the death of their confidant. The one and only individual with which they could share their most secret thoughts and desires is now gone forever, leaving them alone. Depending on the surviving child's age and his or her cognitive ability, this sense of abandonment will be less or more acute. Regardless, if the child were five or twenty-five, they will feel emptiness or abandonment.

A brother twenty-eight years old wrote something to be read at an accident site where a nineteen-year-old driver had killed his twenty-four-year-old brother. His brother had been walking along a roadway when the driver, distracted momentarily for some unknown reason, struck from behind and killed his brother as the vehicle she was driving swerved right. At the roadside memorial, a handmade cross adorned with artificial followers and a photo of the brother was attached along with other pieces and wreaths well placed by a grandmother and two close friends who had joined this surviving brother along with his mother and father, all in acute grief. All took a hand in planting the wild followers that were scattered about, and everyone prayed. It came time for the surviving brother to read his roadside eulogy. Overcome with grief, his father intervened to give a hand, and it read:

"My Brother"

"I have been searching for the things I want to say about my brother, to have others understand him as I did. My brother was my best friend. Every memory of my life includes him for as long as I can remember. For every defining moment of my life I can always see Corey sitting right there next to me. I have never felt so alone in my entire life. Probably because I never have been this alone. Everything he did, he was right there with me whether it was karate, baseball, or in the hard times. He was someone I could confide in and trust that he would always be there for me no matter what. And he was. To me he was the one that would put everyone else's needs in front of his own. He never asked me for hardly anything. He wouldn't burden anyone no matter how bad he needed to talk to someone. He was one of the most unselfish people I have ever met, because be cared more for everyone else than for himself. If anyone was going through a hard time or felt upset or sad about something, he was always the one to tell you a joke or to do something to make the pain you felt go away.

He worked hard so people would be proud of him, no matter what he went through. I can honestly say that no matter what he was going through at that time, I was ALWAYS proud of him. I am honored to say that he was my best friend. Most of all I am HONORED to say that he was MY BROTHER. He was a great friend to everyone he knew. I think everybody has a good story about Corey. He was a wonderful uncle and a very vivid part of the family, a great boss to some, a companion, but there is one thing that no one else in this whole world can say about Corey but me. HE was MY BROTHER! I have found that I was wrong to think that I am alone. I take him with me now, not in person but in my heart. My brother will never be forgotten, and because of that I will never be alone."

Corey on the left, Brian (the author of "My Brother") on the right.

Soon after the loss of a brother or sister, the siblings will become bombarded with emotions that will change their lives forever. One of the strongest of all the emotions for a child has to be guilt. Let's face it: *Leave it to Beaver* and other television programs like it only exist on TV, hardly in real life. While siblings do confide, share, and trust in one another, arguments will erupt, feelings will get hurt, and things will be said; things said in the heat of an argument, in the heat of the moment, things we know we didn't mean. You know the things I am referring to: those words, once spoken, cut like a knife, right into your very soul. You begin to feel remorse soon after the words seem to have fashioned a world of there own, as if they're not yours at all. "Where did they come from? I didn't mean them really, not really at all." You may remember such arguments ending with statements like, "You're not my brother," "I wish you would go away and never come back," "I hate you," or, "I wish you were dead." Soon after the loss of his brother, what was in fact child's play may, if left unattended, become a manifestation to the surviving sibling left with the unrealistic belief that his wish blurted in anger has come true. Now the sibling is feeling responsible for not only the brother's death but also the pain he will see in the eyes all about him.

This is only one example of the many unexplained, unsorted emotions the child must answer themselves on a daily basis. As parents we must, as we always have, pay attention and speak to our remaining children. Let them know they're still safe, even though their world has been fragmented; you're still with them, for them.

Let them know that what happened to their brother or sister they loved so deeply was a tragic event that took all of you by surprise. As parents explain to them that while your lives have changed forever and that we all will feel sad, all will cry, one thing is not to be forgotten: what happened to their brother or sister will not happen to them. They are safe.

On the Road to Healing

For the brother and sister of a lost sibling, please find some comfort in knowing you had a most unique relationship with your brother or sister. You had the closeness of a friend like no other you will ever encounter again in your lifetime, the opportunity to give the gift of love like no other. You will love a wife, a husband, and there too will you be reminded of the trust, confidence, and the loyalties you once shared and now have lost, and as a parent you will see it come full circle. Should you choose to raise children, they too will share and confide and trust and make a pact by stating an oath and crossing their hearts to swear secrecy to one another, and choose not to share the secret with the parents they so dearly strive to please every waking moment. Now you can only hope and pray your children will never endure the lifelong pain of losing a brother or sister, filled with the mature wonder and happy memories of a sibling, a friend of a lifetime, a place where children play, grow, and love like no other, the loving bond of a brother or sister.

ஐ CHAPTER THREE ௸

THE BASKET OF EMOTIONS AND THE BAG OF TOOLS

After twenty-four years devoted to law enforcement, I have encountered many different people from many different walks of life. That includes inside as well as outside the department. The study of human nature, free will vs. predisposition, the complexities of substance abuse and the total destruction that all too often follows, and crisis intervention of every unmanageable magnitude: a new patrol officer will soon be awakened to the realization that law enforcement does not consist of the exciting life betrayed by the "cop" television programs that seem to have flooded the viewing audience of the twentieth and twenty-first century. The new law enforcement officers evolve through a cycle of preconceived notions filled with rotating lights and loud sirens that once activated will cause traffic yield like the parting of the Red Sea. They are answering dispatches to fight calls as well as animal complaints. The world they came to save, to make some significant contribution in, was in fact a fallacy. These new officers find themselves in a battle, not only on the street, placing them at extreme risk only to find ridicule in today's society, threading a multitude of lawsuits at every corner; they also find themselves fighting politics and popular opinion. But what has to be the worst of all is the sense of hopelessness when confronted by the traumatic events in others' lives they encounter in their daily watch while making their rounds within the community they serve.

For me as well, I started my career in law enforcement much the same way. The ego, the power, the bright lights and sirens, and yes, the parting of the sea of the traffic ahead: it was all short lived. I was promoted within the department from patrol officer to detective then to sergeant and supervisor. I never lost sight of my original desire to help others and to make a difference, however naive this may sound to others, for those who know me well know this to be true. I learned very quickly that people in need were falling through the cracks. Recognition of families in crisis and the way in which law enforcement recruits were being trained to confront individuals in crisis was falling short by a long shot. I knew that by pushing a referral into the hand of a person in need, they were quietly being escorted out the door with a few kind words. This did nothing to comfort and provide the support they needed. These people were only recently confronted with the devastation of a lifetime. They needed some direction in which to start; a path to follow, with a few kind words of encouragement from someone they knew really cared and would be there for them at the drop of a hat if they needed it. Sometimes the simplest of kind words can make a tremendous difference if presented at the right time with an intelligent reference, and that includes knowing when to just sit, be quiet, and listen. So, not to insult your intelligence, my friends, but allow me to suggest that I have just given you a tool, one of many to come as we explore this very important chapter of emotions and the tools you will need to make sense of it all.

This brief chapter is, by its design, an aid to help explain what is innate in all of us. It is a concept that has served me well for many years in counseling individuals and their families in crisis. As we begin to explore, you will soon recognize that "the basket of emotions and the bag of tools" is a simple concept of dissection and organization of the many complicated emotions that have recently been dropped in your lap at the worst possible time in your life. To some degree or another, for each of us it is nothing more than life's experiences of learning that enable us to cope and solve our day-to-day challenges and conflicts. For some of us, during this very difficult time we may not recognize they exist under a specific name or theory. But the tools we have acquired through our life's experiences are second nature to us in that, as we mature, as we resolve our conflicts we will have learned a new life experience. By doing so, we have acquired a new tool. This tool is placed in our memory for future use. Those tools we find successful we save, and the tools we discover less effective we discard. Very often this is referred to as trial and error.

THE BAG OF TOOLS

As we begin our early childhood lives we depend on others for their support, their nurturing, and their protection. We develop through childhood into the teenage years filled with our own set of challenges in the different stages of adolescence and continue into adulthood and all too soon into what is lightly labeled the *golden years*. In these transitions on life's journey, we walk a path filled with many twist and turns, crossroads that lead in many different directions. As we approach each of these we face a decision that will latently determine the course of our lives. For each and every one of us, it's always the same: we have choices to make that will affect the rest of our lives with the snowball effect for generations to follow. We will discuses this path in great detail in the chapter on faith.

As we continue on life's path filled with hopes, dreams, and aspirations, we experience an array of obstacles along the way, and as we stumble and fall, we pick ourselves back up, brush ourselves off, and go about our way, continuing with the promise of a new learning experience just around the corner. But you must recognize that each time you have fallen and experienced a new challenge, you acquired a new tool to place in your bag of tools. This bag of tools you carry with you always; it never leaves your side. It's always there for you to draw from, to pick from, to choose that special tool to help you, enable you to fix a problem in your life or fix a problem for someone else. It is truly a gift, a gift from God. As we go on with this bag of tools it becomes heavier and heavier but never burdensome. Each turn you take on your path, each fork in the road you chouse, you acquire a new and precious tool. These tools are as valued as life itself. They are your trials and errors. Without the recognition that the tool exists, the problem will go on unrecognized, not dealt with, unresolved.

BASKET OF EMOTIONS

As we discussed in chapter one on grief, soon after the notification of the sudden death of your child and the denial that follows, this basket of emotions drops in your lap. It totally overcomes you; it disables you and leaves you as a shell of the person you were only hours ago. It seems like a lifetime. This again is acute grief, and soon we discover that we are not alone. We have others in our lives who are suffering and who are looking for our direction. However helpless we feel, however sick and overcome we are, they will come to us for the support and the love they so desperately need. They will lack the understanding of it all and so will you, but you may have the one thing they don't, the one thing they lack: the tool to help them sort. You won't have all the answers; you can't be expected to make sense of this tragic event, so don't even try. Just tell them that you're there for them and that you will all get through this with each other's support. Be there to hold each other, to cry with each other. By consoling one another on this road never traveled, you will need each others comforting presence. As time permits, explain the basket of emotions to them and be honest with them that this is something you haven't worked out yet yourself. It will most likely be some time before your family can start healing, but let them know that you're there for them, and ask them to be there for you. Tell them you need them too; this will give them a sense of helping instead of abandonment.

This newly discovered basket of emotions is full. It's stacked one on top of another; it's totally confusing and complicated. If left in this state little can be resolved and acute grief will be unnecessarily prolonged more than it would if this burden could only be sorted to a more manageable and segmented value. By this I mean with the bag of tools at your side and when you feel you're ready to set the basket in front of you and begin the task of sorting. There are so many emotions such as guilt, fear, faith, unrealistic expectations, anger, denial—all to be addressed in the next chapter—that you will continue to be overcome and unable to adequately deal with the emotions that are mentally and physically effecting your every waking moment.

My analogy of the basket of emotions and the bag of tools is not intended to insult your intelligence. It is only my simplistic example, passed on to you with the hopeful intention that it may define what you already know, and by doing so bring your gifts (tools) into your conscious mindset, first to help yourself, then hopefully for you to pass on to your loved ones, giving them the understanding that they too possess the tools that will enable them to sort their own baskets.

Keep in mind, my friends, that after you sort your emotions and you have the tool to begin dealing with the emotion at hand, one by one, these feelings may not soon disappear. You will find that some of your emotions are easier to address than others are and that there will be some that we will have to battle all our remaining years. However, understand that each and every one of your emotions can be dissected and understood to some manageable degree. Remember, as pointed out in the first chapter on grief, that if you feel you're not dealing with your loss within your own time frame you must bring yourself to the reasonable understanding that you may need assistance. Seek out a qualified counselor, make the appointment, and keep it no matter what; make no excuses, go seek help, and you will begin to start coping better as you continue with any recommended follow-up appointments. For some it may only require one or two meetings; for others the visits may need to continue. The important thing to remember is that no two individuals are the same. We all muddle through on our own timetable, and no single rule applies to everyone.

So without delay let us briefly explore the basic emotions that plague our progress to a better existence and the goal of a healthier life.

෯ CHAPTER FOUR ଔ

EMOTIONS

As we begin to explore some of the emotions acutely associated after the tragic and sudden loss of your child or sibling, we need to understand that not everyone involved with this devastation in our lives will feel the turmoil to the same degree as others. On the other hand, there will be emotions that we will share with our loved ones, such as shock, acute grief, grief, anger, and fear, just to mention a few. During this chapter, I will spare you the complex areas of theology, philosophy, and the scientific terminology associated with psychology regarding human relations and individual personalities. This chapter is intended to be a broad introductory overview of some basic emotions associated with our loss. I chose to continue to write to you in the personal manner in which I have attempted thus far, parent to parent.

GUILT

Choosing guilt to be first on the list to discuss is not a random, unconscious thought. Guilt and anger have to be the strongest heartfelt emotions we have to confront after we find ourselves in grief.

The could-haves, the should-haves, etc., we could go on and on if we allow ourselves to do so. Please, my dear friends, understand that for every action there is a reaction, and let's not play God. I believe that to some degree we will continue to question our motives and our many mistakes along the way. But we must recognize that we brought our children into this world in our younger years with little or no experience at all. Our children arrived with a book filled with blank pages for us to write on. We're going to make mistakes, and a lot of them. No one is excluded; not even the greatest minds on this planet can raise a child without making mistakes, some of the same mistakes you and I have made in the past. Mistakes like having said things we wish we had not and, more important, the things we wish we had.

There are many things we as caring loving parents can recall without effort that cut deep into our souls and bring us to tears and overwhelming sadness. Personally I remember informing my sons that after high school graduation they had three choices: they could continue their education and attend collage; they could obtain full-time employment, or they could enter the military. I made it clear that they would not become couch potatoes, sleeping till noon every day; they had to develop a productive existence. On its face we know this is sound parental advice given in the proper format with the correct encouragement. After the loss of this child, though, if we allow ourselves we may distort this reasonable request into a means to an end and find ourselves feeling guilty, as though we might have put too much pressure on the child, forcing him or her to leave the house in defiance.

If you suffer with such feelings, let us discuss some facts you may have temporarily placed on the back burner. The fact is, my friends, we grew up in a different generation. A generation where jobs were scarce and the wages low. We were forced many times to worry about paying the bills and keeping food on the table and clothing on our children's backs. For the majority of us it took many years to develop our careers to a comfortable state where we had a positive cash flow with the ability to save a few bucks for our children's education, better clothing, and a few extras such as a swimming pool or maybe that new bike the kids wanted.

For the parents who had to endure the worst of times, as my history lessons have thought me, they who struggled to survive during the Depression may say we as the "baby boomers" have spoiled our children with unnecessary gifts and allowances (monetary or otherwise), to which I can only reply, thank God for the blessing. Speaking for the overwhelming majority in the middle class of the twentieth century, I wish I could have done more, saved more, spent more quality time with my family, and worked less (a little of my own guilt?).

SURVIVOR'S GUILT

In the beginning, soon after our loss, we experience what is known as survivor's guilt. We ask ourselves, and God, "Why, why couldn't it have been me? I am so much older then he. Why was I spared only to lose my child, who left this world with so many unfulfilled dreams and expectations, the opportunity to express themselves, to understand true love, and to live life in the fullest?" From infancy through childhood development, the wants and wishes will be derived from ourselves as parents. We will develop our own expectations for our children, as they exist in a world of their own with their own concerns and desires. They may consume their time with the desires of playtime and uncomplicated interaction with parents, siblings, and friends. The birthday party of a neighborhood playmate will become a major event in their lives with the simple rewards of cake and ice cream as well as the wonderful gifts they will give concealed in beautiful wrapping paper.

As for the adolescent, the young adult, they will begin developing their own dreams and personal goals. Their timelines for themselves are filled with expectations and desires that fill their lives with happiness and the prosperity of a lifetime choosing for themselves, and we as parents will embrace their wishes with open arms. As their lives come to an end, we the parents will soon discover the unfairness of it all. We will ask ourselves again and again, why could it not have been me instead? We have lived our lives the best we could, now why has this child been robbed of their chance at life? Survivor's guilt in acute grief, or PTSD, can be overwhelming without the understanding that will come very soon, if at all. We will, however, in time develop some type of acceptance to one degree or another. Why? Because we have to.

Tom, a good friend of mine, recently shared with me that, while some will exceed life's expectancy, contributing little, there will be others taken from this earth long before their time but who that have given greatness. Their short lives have had such a positive impact on those they encountered in their short time that they will never be forgotten; rather, they will be remembered with kindness, admiration, love, and the grateful joy of our child having been a part in their own lives. The gifts our child left behind, the unselfish kindness, love, and joy will be welcome reminders for parents, siblings, and other family members as well as the friends who may find themselves in conflict with the many emotions yet dissected. They will find some relief knowing that even a child can make great contributions in the lives of others.

Remembering what we have learned in the previous chapters—that some will say and do things without understanding—so it will be true for some who will take pen in hand and write without understanding. We will read with disbelief as we find ourselves in conflict with some who have chosen to present their untested theories in the face of our society as well as our personal lives. However unpleasant, it will remain our choice to keep what we find reasonable and discard the rest; the following will provide a sound example.

There is a current controversy ongoing within our society these days that seems to have manifested itself with such disbelief it clearly defies definition. It began in 1991 when a man named Douglas Coupland wrote a fiction novel stereotyping and labeling our youth born between the years 1965 and 1980 as generation "X." Bear with me, for I wish to discuss with you this issue, which I promise will have a meaning and understanding. This problematic, stereotypical, labeling and actuation of accusing our children of being slackers, unwilling to work for their own future rewards, may be disturbing at best. Like those who speak loudly on this subject, I can only support their objections with great vigor. The youth today are tomorrow's future and do not get the credit they deserve.

For the young adults today plagued with the obstacles in their everyday life, such as peer pressure, the abundance and acceptance of drugs, and the sexual revolution, as some would like to call it, they now are faced with being labeled the "X" generation, meaning that they lack the true understanding of our predecessors and what it means to work their way up the ladder, as their parents and forefathers had before them. The study seems to imply that the youth of today have lived a higher standard and therefore have developed this standard as a common place to start in the workplace with or without an education. As these controversies continue they have found it necessary to rename this new and upcoming generation the "Y" generation, with the same fundamentals as the "X" generation only with a new age group and a revision in expectations.[1]

There is a method to my madness. The reason why I have to bring this controversy to your attention is that whether you agree with it or not, we as loving and caring parents develop expectations for our children. We want the best for them. We don't want them to struggle through life. We want better for them. We begin to reinforce in early childhood when asking our children, "Do you want to be a doctor? Or maybe a lawyer? An engineer perhaps?" We find in most cases children want to become policemen or firefighters, an action figure they have recently been exposed to at a school function, or during a school-sponsored fieldtrip to a local fire house where they climbed on the many different vehicles, or walking through the police station meeting. The police chief takes a group of children on a tour of the lockup facilities, where all the bad guys are locked up for their protection, and later they sit in the police squad car and activate the lights and siren. As a parent it will be hard to compete with such stimuli. At least for now. My point is, my friends, that we do and have developed expectations for our children, some we have to admit are "unrealistic expectations" that we impose on our children, who, as we have previously learned, want nothing more than to please us in every way.

As I mentioned earlier, the regrets we share, the could-haves, should-haves, and the mistakes along the way, from young parents to the mistakes made in middle age, need to be reinforced in a positive way, understanding that these are feelings of guilt that can be distorted as tragedy enters our lives. The majority of our regrets may become difficult to manage and understand if we fail to take a step back and intelligently examine this emotion with fairness to other family members and friends as well as ourselves. The grieving cycle is going to be a complicated, lifelong event. If we allow this emotion to take control, it can and probably will regress our healing progress to the point of an unnecessary value by distorting our true feelings and the closeness we so carefully nurtured during our child's development. We need to remind ourselves over and over again if necessary that we are not God and that mistakes are going to be made as we walk along this road less traveled, with kindness to others as well as ourselves, on the way to a healthier mind and body. It is important to recognize that unmanaged guilt can also distort the many other emotions that have filled our basket and are yet to be discussed.

Anger

The *Scott Foresman Advanced Dictionary*, complied by E. L. Thorndike and Clarence L. Barnhart, 1979, defines anger as "the feeling one has toward something or someone that hurts, opposes, offends, or annoys; strong displeasure; wrath."

After digesting the definition above, those of us in grief may consider it a gross understatement at best. As we search for some reasonable understanding and explanation as to how and why such devastation has claimed our child, we may find ourselves angry at the world as well as our God (explained in chapter six on faith). Not only will we be angry with ourselves, we may find ourselves angry at an array of institutions and individuals. Wrath (or rage) kept unchecked can and often will prove to be misguided and at times unfair. The destructive qualities of rage can be devastating for ourselves and those around us as well as some misguided target.

After the tragic and sudden loss of a child, we will undoubtedly strive for the answers that led to the events that claimed our child, and this is more than understandable. We must, however, keep our goals in focus without allowing the qualities of anger and rage to consume us. We as human beings need to understand that our thoughts, actions, and personalities are driven by our emotions, whether it be recognized and understood within the conscious or the subconscious mind, free from neuroses associated with abnormal psychology. As we study our emotions academically within psychology, we will discover that the ongoing scientific research influencing the many different writings of others makes strong reference to their theories and interpretations, which are found to be similar in nature with regard to a healthy self and that of abnormality.

Condition Responses

Now that we have discussed the top three emotions related to the loss of a child, we need to understand and recognize how they, if left unattended, may intrude upon us as we strive for a healthier self. Symptoms are well recognized as a noticeable change in the normal working of the body and mind that indicates or accompanies disease. Symptoms or aliments will be the result of unattended emotions that have yet to be properly dissected and addressed. It is only through self-realization that we will acknowledge that a problem may exist within ourselves as well as others.

I have mentioned previously, and will continue to do so, that if we recognize abnormalities in behavior we must seek help from a qualified M.D., Ph.D., counselor, or that of a support group that deals with grief after the loss of a child. Again, not all physicians, clinical therapists, psychiatrists, or behaviorist counselors are created equal. All enter their chosen professions as caregivers addressing the physical, mental, and spiritual needs of individuals they encounter. All of these caregivers will derive a particular specialty as they develop within their professions, and to believe that each and every one of them has developed the tools needed to relate to those of us after such a catastrophic tragedy is an attitude we cannot afford to have: the compliancy and luxury to predetermine that our needs will be met by just choosing our guide by way of the Yellow Pages. We must take personal responsibility when choosing a provider, if not for ourselves then for others who may not recognize a change within their own thoughts and behaviors. When you begin your search, feel free to ask questions and inform them of what you're facing as well your concerns and feelings and your desire to achieve some reasonable understanding, striving for that healthier self or that of a loved one. Our lives have changed forever: this is an undeniable fact. It will remain within us on our journey for the rest of our lives filled with the many emotions and triggers that will at times send us back, back in time, as if this time in our lives has stood still. It is not, I repeat, not abnormal as we feel the pain and despair after the loss of our children, my dear friends. Know that you're not going nuts nor are you on your way to that funny farm. You're not alone. All who have encountered a parent's worst nightmare will give testimony to the above that is with time, a lot of time, that we will become healthy survivors as well as living examples as we reiterate our own travels behind us as well as those we may face on a daily basis looking into the future. Within the following we will examine some of the symptoms and aliments that hopefully will lead us in the correct direction as we seek help in addressing some of the emotions we encounter. Let us recognize with reinforcement, the promise of a healthier self, that within our own time frame we will endure. Beginning with the most extreme of these we will continue the delicate process of dissection.

Post-Traumatic Stress Disorder

Post-Traumatic Stress Disorder (PTSD) will first be recognized within shock and into acute grief. This disorder is the result of a traumatic, disastrous event with extreme pain that has severe psychological and physiological challenges. Following a life-changing traumatic event, such as in the loss of a child, we, the parents and siblings, will become the unwelcome recipients filled with despair and denial. PTSD is not to be confused within the many stages of depression or that of sadness. PTSD is a disabling condition that can be recognized within yourself and others as actions that are not considered normal within the individual. An example could be that of reclusiveness; the inability to perform everyday tasks such as tending to one's personal hygiene; extreme sleep disorders; lack of appetite; or despondence. If you suspect that you or someone you love is displaying any of these characteristics, please seek immediate intervention. This can be an extremely dangerous condition that can only be properly diagnosed by a professional. It is my strong advice that this fear be met without delay.

Depression

Just as PTSD is not to be confused with depression, so it is that depression should not be confused with sadness. Within any physician's office you'll find several pamphlets addressing any number of aliments or news of current health issues and that will provide information on an array of concerns. Depression is to be recognized as unavoidable after the tragic and sudden loss of a child, not only for parents and siblings, but also to all who have had the privilege of developing a close relationship with our child. We will be reminded of this later in chapter seven, describing and recognizing other family members and loving friends, as they too will experience difficulties as the loss of a child will resonate within their cultivated relationships.

One of these pamphlets I speak of addresses depression as "not just feeling down; it is a real medical condition that can be effectively treated."[2]

I recommend that you copy the following self-rating test and if you feel the need, ask your loved one to take the quiz. Should you discover that you or they score within the guidelines of depression, please bring the self-test to a professional who is trained to determine the severity through consultation. Let us begin by circling the number that best describes you for the past seven days.

One. Falling asleep:
0. I never take longer than 30 minutes to fall asleep.
1. I take at least 30 minutes to fall asleep, less than half the time.
2. I take at least 30 minutes to fall asleep, more than half the time.
3. I take more than 60 minutes to fall asleep, more than half the time.

Two. Sleep during the night:
0. I do not wake up at night.
1. I have a restless, light sleep with a few brief awakenings each night.
2. I wake up at least once a night, but go back to sleep easily.
3. I awaken more than once a night and stay awake for 20 minutes or more, more than half the time.

Three. Waking up too early:

0. Most of the time, I awaken no more than 30 minutes before I need to get up.
1. More than half the time, I awaken more than 30 minutes before I need to get up.
2. I almost always awaken at least one hour or so before I need to, but I go back to sleep eventually.
3. I awaken at least one hour before I need to, and can't go back to sleep.

Four. Sleeping too much:

0. I sleep no more than 7-8 hours a night, without napping during the day.
1. I sleep no more than 10 hours in a 24-hour period including naps.
2. I sleep no more than 12 hours in a 24-hour period including naps.
3. I sleep more than 12 hours in a 24-hour period including naps.

Five. Feeling sad:

0. I do not feel sad.
1. I feel sad less than half the time.
2. I feel sad more than half the time.
3. I feel sad nearly all the time.

Six. Decreased appetite:

0. There is no change in my usual appetite.
1. I eat somewhat less often or lesser amounts of food than usual.
2. I eat much less than usual and only with personal effort.
3. I rarely eat within a 24-hour period, and only with extreme personal effort or when others persuade me to eat.

Seven. Increased appetite:

0. There is no change from my usual appetite.
1. I feel a need to eat more frequently than usual.
2. I regularly eat more often and/or greater amounts of food than usual.
3. I feel driven to overeat both at mealtime and between meals.

Eight. Decreased weight (within the last two weeks):

0. I have not had any change in my weight.
1. I feel as if I've had a slight weight loss.
2. I have lost 2 pounds or more.
3. I have lost 5 pounds or more.

Nine. Increased weight (within the last two weeks):

0. I have not had any change in my weight.
1. I feel as if I've had a slight weight gain.
2. I have gained 2 pounds or more.
3. I have gained 5 pounds or more.

Ten. Concentration/Decision making:

0. There is no change in my usual capacity to concentrate or make decisions.
1. I occasionally feel indecisive or find that my attention wanders.
2. Most of the time, I struggle to focus my attention or to make decisions.
3. I cannot concentrate well enough to read or cannot make even minor decisions.

Eleven. View of myself:

0. I see myself as equally worthwhile and deserving as other people.
1. I am more self-blaming than usual.

2. I largely believe that I cause problems for others.

3. I think almost constantly about major and minor defects in myself.

Twelve. Thoughts of death or suicide:

0. I do not think of suicide or death.

1. I feel that life is empty or wonder if it's worth living.

2. I think of suicide or death several times a week for several minutes.

3. I think of suicide or death several times a day in some detail, or I have made specific plans for suicide or have actually tried to take my own life.

Thirteen. General interest:

0. There is no change from usual in how interested I am in other people or activities.

1. I notice that I am less interested in people or activities.

2. I find I have interest in only one or two of my formerly pursued activities.

3. I have virtually no interest in formerly pursued activities.

Fourteen. Energy level:

0. There is no change in my usual level of energy.

1. I get tired more easily than usual.

2. I have to make a big effort to start or finish my usual daily activities.

3. I really cannot carry out most of my usual daily activities because I just don't have the energy.

Fifteen. Feeling slowed down:

0. I think, speak, and move at my usual rate of speed.

1. I find that my thinking is slowed down or my voice sounds dull of flat.

2. It takes me several seconds to respond to most questions, and I'm sure my thinking is slowed.
3. I am often unable to respond to questions without extreme effort.

Sixteen. Feeling restless:

0. I do not feel restless.
1. I'm often fidgety, wringing my hands, or need to shift while I'm sitting.
2. I have impulses to move about and I'm quite restless.
3. At times I am unable to stay seated and need to pace around.

Scoring Criteria:

0-5: Normal

6-10: Mild

11-15: Moderate

16-20: Severe

21+: Very Severe

Again, how you may score yourself is in my opinion only an indicator. If you find yourself uncomfortable being aware of where you are, you are well advised to bring this self-test to a qualified professional for advice and/or treatment. Please do yourself as well as others a favor and do it without delay.

Sadness

There are as many degrees of sadness as there are in depression. After the loss of a child, sadness will take on a new meaning, unlike normal sadness, which affects everyone within this complicated world. Simply put, for those individuals free of the devastation of a lifetime suffering in the acute, sadness can be related within a broad array of conditions. The change of seasons, weather, lack of sunshine, or rain, just to mention a few, can intrude upon those diagnosed with Seasonal Affective Disorder (SAD) who may be diagnosed in the low to severe range due to SAD. To use an example, many will feel the "blues" during the winter months as the days become shorter and the sky remains cloudy most of the season. I personally became aware of SAD during what is referred to as the "winter blues" and how it came to affect my wife, who, as it turned out, was being affected by the lack of ultraviolet rays (sunshine). My wife was affected for several years, and with every passing year it seemed to intensify to the point that she told me that she just felt "lazy and lacked motivation." I just wrote it off as a time in her life when most women entered the beginning stages of menopause. It was not until the next year during a psychology class in which we approached "seasonal disorders" that I learned that what she was experiencing largely was not due to menopause. That Christmas she received a three-month subscription to a tanning salon. Within a week of treatment she showed significant improvement, and she now receives this gift annually, in one form or another. This general example recognizes sadness within the lifespan as that which is readily accepted as normal. This being said, in some cases sadness, if left unattended and unrecognized, can develop into depression if not properly diagnosed by a professional. This remains extremely important for anyone who finds him or herself in any type of grief.

Anxiety

The symptoms of anxiety will vary from one person to the next. From "basic anxiety" to what is referred to as "panic disorder." I have to believe that everyone will discover basic anxiety throughout one's lifespan as we develop cognitively, emotionally, physically, and spiritually. This has to be recognized as normal and free of neurosis. How can this not be true for us, first as children who strive to gain approval from caregivers and then as we enter early adulthood and later become mature adults, developing our own personal life goals and expectations, whether they are realistic or unrealistic?

As we evolve from the essential stages of grieving, first found in shock then into the stages of grieving to follow, acute grief or PTSD, then into grief and the many triggers that send us to and fro, simple anxiety will follow after several years have past as we become aware of the anniversary dates as the years slowly pass. This will become welcome during the healing process, as we never forget our loss, becoming aware that those that surround us do. Such is true for a lady named Gertrude.

As a survivor, Gertrude came to the realization, free of denial, that once some time ago her life was filled with despair and confusion.

Gertrude K., a lady now in her eighties, residing in the Midwest, shares a story of her own that proves to be a strong example. As she entered into the bond of marriage with Joseph in 1945 they brought forth four loving gifts from God. First came Ken, followed by Rick, Karen, and their youngest, Mary Beth. This wonderful lady had known despair throughout her life with the passing of several family members and friends, to which all of us can relate with compassion and understanding. Now with health issues of her own, she will arrive when called upon by others to comfort with her kind, loving ways for which she will take little credit herself as she reminds others that it is not within her, but through the guidance of God. My family is the grateful beneficiary of this strong, faithful, loving family that words cannot truly describe.

In 1982, Gertrude became aware of the second strongest stressor life has to endure when her one and only true love and soul mate, Joseph, passed in the physical, leaving her with the gifts of the children that to this day surround her with their strong values and faith, which they continue to receive as reinforcements by example, past and present. While still in acute grief after the passing of her husband, Joseph, despair reentered her life as well as her children's when the first and foremost stressor of a lifetime occurred. Her youngest child, Mary Beth, at the young age of twenty-three, after years of battling it, succumbed to Hodgkin's disease in 1984. Now, after several years of separation in the physical, this woman gives thanks to her Lord and God for the many joyful memories she continually recognizes as blessings and gifts she observers within the eyes of her remaining children and grandchildren. While a tear will still fall upon her face as she encounters the triggers and trials that face her daily, she embraces the moments of those wonderful, joyful days long past that seem to stand still in time as her anxiety finds her at every approaching anniversary date.

Pain

Whether it is psychological or physical, the "pain" is as real as life itself. For all of us who have lost a loved one—husband, wife, parent, sibling, as well as the extreme, a child—will not escape the effects of real pain within the body and soul. We will soon discover that a piece of us is missing, a piece within the heart. It will not be difficult to recognize within ourselves or in the others we will encounter along life's path. Please, my dear friends, be kind to those you will encounter. Their trails and tribulations will not be open for discussion. They will appear to be callous, even uncomfortable to be around. Try to understand that some of those we encounter will be in despair and unknowingly present themselves within their true light. They may be totally unaware of their actions due to the fact that they lack true understanding themselves. Be kind to all you encounter, knowing that unless you have walked a mile in their shoes, you will have no way of knowing where they have been or where they're going. Sound familiar?

Again God bless and lead you upon this road less traveled.

☙ CHAPTER FIVE ❧

MEMORIALS

Memorials come in many shapes and forms. For some of us, as the parents and siblings, they are as necessary as life itself. It is so important that we recognize our lost one, as it is for our own survival in this life filled with the many emotions that drive us to honor our child in some type of everlasting tribute of affection. We need to bring meaning to and show recognition of the life that has once enlightened our hearts and souls with their existence filled with joy and happiness. What has been lost in the physical has now been replaced in the spiritual. We will strive to understand our devastating loss and in some way help make sense of it all.

Shortly after the loss of our child, we find ourselves in the early stages of grief. We may find a need to surround ourselves with items that remind us of our child. Some of us will arrange our favorite pictures that hold special meaning for us. These well-placed photos about our home will serve as daily reminders that in some small way we are still connected. The long weeks and months will pass and the daily reminders will become less painful. We become aware that at some date in the future a well thought out tribute to share with others will be at hand.

The roadsides these days are abundant with memorials that mark the area where a child was lost due to an automobile incident. The roadside crosses that identify the site where a loved one was taken from us serve as a temporary reminder. Later as time begins the slow process of healing, we will discover a more permanent memorial is needed, allowing us a time and place to honor and remember our child.

A sibling tells me of a roadside memorial he constructed in memory of his younger brother as a place where he could come and visit. He stated that this was a place where he could find comfort; he can be with his brother in meditation unencumbered by the demands of others. A place where he can reflect upon the gifts that his loving brother gave, not just to himself, but also to the many others that knew his brother well. This site where his brother took his last breath on earth now servers as a place frozen, suspended in time, where he can sit peacefully to spend time with is brother, where he can speak with the brother knowing that this is a place where he and his brother can somehow converse spiritually. On bended knee he will pray to God for comfort and peace, remembering the many cherished memories that they have to share, a bond of a lifetime.

Memorials

Memorials are healthy tools that provide comfort for you and your loved ones and in some cases can bring a scheduled, well-structured, and maintained place in time for all who wish to participate.

Others will find comfort at a burial site where their child was placed to rest. The cemeteries throughout the world will ever so gently hold the shell that our child once occupied, the body that served our child as a vessel to contain the real self of our loved one, the spirit that will live forever. In the beginning, visits to our memorials are frequent reminders filled with the gifts our child has given us: the joy and happiness as well as the many reminders of a wonderful smile, the loving embrace, and the pride of knowing that this child had provided an everlasting contribution in our lives. Also, others will remember our child with fond recollections of respect and the love they too will cherish the remaining years of their lives.

I know of a mother that purchased a cultured stone that was engraved with an inscription that best reflected the admiration she first knew in the real self (the body) and now in the everlasting soul that will await her in heaven, in the presence of God. It read:

If tears could build a stairway,
And memories a lane,
I'd walk right up to heaven and bring you home again.
(Author unknown)

A Place and Time

Depending on the circumstances that surround our loss, we will search for the ways that will provide a much-needed healthy environment to honor our child within our own comfort zone. Whether it be the roadside memorial or a gravesite, this place will serve as a healthy atmosphere for years, as the site will lure the family and loving friends of ours as well as the close friends of our children. Our hearts will go out to the families and friends who find themselves without such a place that I have just described. Over the years many children have been lost, reported missing, and, for some, the children have yet to be discovered and are presumed dead.

Remember also those young men and women that have served in the military defending our country and who have been sent overseas to some distant land, as our country demands. They have been called to serve by our government and will be placed them within a war or conflict for a large variety of reasons. Some of these reasons are easily accepted as a necessity to secure and protect our country and those populations in other countries where their citizens may find themselves facing the threat of tyranny or genocide, similar to what we in the United States found to be true during the Second World War. Our children in these cases are soldiers called upon take a weapon in hand to an uncertain destiny.

Some of these brave souls will be reported missing in action or casualties of war never to be returned to their families, who are forced to wait, praying for their safe return. Arlington National Cemetery is one of several national memorial cemeteries within the United States dedicated to honoring our war heroes and veterans alike. The sites in Arlington, Virginia, currently hold more than 260,000 burial sites and add approximately 140 new graves a week. Close to four million people will visit the cemetery and the Tomb of the Unknown Soldier in Arlington annually to pay their last respects to loved ones and friends. In addition to the burial sites, there are many other memorials that serve as places of remembrance but that do not contain any physical remains due to the fact that those listed are missing in action and these lost ones remain un-recovered, for one reason or another, due to the catastrophic tragedies associated with war. The sense of emptiness can only be fully recognized by those who suffer such a loss.

I have friends residing in Wisconsin who also own a cottage on a lake in a remote rural area of central Wisconsin. As neighbors on this lake, we developed a relationship that I truly cherish. A cottage is a place where a family can visit or reside that will provide the benefits of a remote second home filled with countless memories as we enjoy our loved ones, young and old alike, who will take advantage of the many gifts and wonders of the quiet countryside. The bright stars that adorn the sky with such brilliance will not be ignored. We as parents will always remember the wide-eyed, enormous smiles of family and guests that arrive for a visit as they begin to discover their personal path filled with the experiences embedded forever in the minds and souls of the fortunate at a place where they will enjoy the extravagant blessings of God. For those of you who have yet to obtain a getaway home away from home, leaving the rat race behind, I offer my advice that you too can rearrange your priorities and fulfill a dream you will not regret, providing an atmosphere that all will surely enrich the lives of your loved ones forever. The purpose for my sharing this factual story with you will soon be revealed in the text on offering a place and time to be enjoyed in the present rather than the future.

Soon after Don, his wife, Marilynn, and myself developed our friendship, I was told of their son Tom, twenty-eight years old. Tom was reported missing in July of 1992. Tom was a soldier serving in the U.S. Navy as a pilot. One day while flying a routine mission over the Atlantic Ocean, the plane he was flying left the radar screen; this plane as well as the crew has yet to be located or recovered. The parents, Don and Marilynn, will continue to speak of their child with kind, loving remembrances as they describe the unfolding events that led to their loss, as well as the emotions they encounter without their son's body being returned for a proper burial. The emptiness in their lives is not with total despair. They can reflect upon the many memories of their child that enhance the wonderful joy they shared with their son at the cottage and elsewhere. Today there is a small, well-placed stone on the cottage property that is engraved, "In Loving Memory of Tom." This stone serves as one of their memorials in tribute to the son lost in body but not in spirit.

Whenever Don was not at his cottage, I would look after his place and he did the same for me. I cannot remember a time while checking on Don's place that I failed to walk over to this stone and reflect upon their loss as well as my own. Remembering our children comes to all of us with little effort. With a well-placed memorial honoring our child comes the satisfaction of knowing that our children will not be forgotten in the eyes of others who will look upon this memorial as they too reflect upon the loss of a child, whether they knew our child or not. It wills them to a conscious state of mind that these tragedies can happen to anyone and that it's not just something that affects others. So you see, my dear friends, a memorial is not just self-serving; rather, it serves as a reminder for so many others who will develop a renewed awareness of the reality of mortality, just as we have come to know that heaven is not only a place for the gray and old.

There are as many different memorials these days as there are childhood deaths. Some may be similar in nature, but each and every one will hold an element of personalization that will distinguish one from another. For those who have never lost a child in their lives, they may drive or walk by a memorial paying little or no attention at all, and this comes with good understanding. Childhood deaths in the United States are reported in the overwhelming minority. The table below reflects the numbers of the leading causes of childhood deaths in this country in the most resent study reported by the U.S. Census Bureau, 1992.[3]

Cause	Age 1-14	Age 15-24
Accidents	6,900	16,700
Cancer (Malignant neoplasms)	1,700	1,900
Congenital anomalies	1,400	—
Homicide	900	6,200
Suicide	—	4,900
Heart disease	600	900
Pneumonia and influenza	400	—
HIV infection	—	600
All other causes	4,300	5,300
Totals	16,200	36,500

As we can plainly see, the numbers reflect the fact that childhood deaths are minimal in comparison to the total current mortality rate of 2,469,125 per year (reported by the U.S. Census Bureau, 2001).

For all who have come upon the road less traveled after the loss of a child, passing by a memorial will attract our attention in a state of awareness. As we recognize their loss we will also become reacquainted with our own. All family members and friends that may walk this path will feel the effects of others; these family members and friends will at times be taken off guard, their minds preoccupied with their own reflections of life's challenges and concerns. They will stumble upon a variety of these memorials, and they will ever so slightly bow their heads in sadness for the unknown families and their lost children as well as their own.

Those of us who find ourselves in grief after losing a child will enter into a subculture within our society unlike the many subcultures that distinguish between race, ethnicity, or origin. Whether we choose to embrace it or not, we will soon recognize a common bond with which we alone can relate. Friendships may develop as we strive to share the memories of our child with someone who can truly relate.

Many friends and family will visit children known to them in the oncology wards at hospitals throughout the country, and as they do so they will pass a memorial in the form of a bulletin board where photographs are placed in remembrance of the children that succumbed to the unkind, unfair illnesses that have infected their young, tender bodies.

Flowers will appear to be abundant not only within the many rooms in the ward but also adorning the hallways and nurse's stations, given with the most sincere thank-yous to the medical staff that will, or that have, provided the loving attention given to the children. Some of these children will survive the immediate threat of the many illnesses of their affliction, but there will be others who will not. The family and friends who walk the hallways during their visits shall take notice of the patients as they lay upon their hospital beds, or observe other children walking the hallways, rolling their personal metal stands that hold the plastic bags that administer the drugs and nutrients by way of an intravenous injection. Visitors will take notice of the many children as well as the different stages of their illnesses. Some of the children will appear docile and pale, while so many others will greet visitors known to them as well as the other strangers with a waving little hand and a large smile. The visitors, family, and friends will not be alone as they feel their heartstrings being tugged with despair and helplessness. God bless the caregivers. With strong conviction and desire they render aid and relief to these children. Also bless the physicians, nursing staff, and those who volunteer as well as the many others within the healthcare profession worldwide for they will not be spared the emotions that will take all of them to that place in time filled with discomfort (to put it mildly).

I remember a warm day in July 1978 shortly after the birth of my second child Curtis. He was born approximately two weeks premature; he was well attended to in that small, isolated room next to the maternity ward. This room was surrounded by glass with blinds on pull-strings that could be lowered and closed for privacy.

The mother, my wife, was heavily sedated, lying on her bed in and out of sleep within her recovery room. I will never forget the events as they came to unfold. My wife, Sharon, was surrounded by her loving family, who sat and stood awaiting the good news in anticipation of welcoming this child into the family. I, on the other hand, found myself standing in the hallway as I watched our new baby in distress.

I remember the attention given by the physician that would come in and out of this small room and the nurses that never left our child's side. The doctor would monitor the child, reading the chart then glancing at me with a look of concern. It wasn't long before this doctor would approach me with the news that our child was in distress due to an undeveloped internal organ. The doctor stood next to me answering the many questions I imposed upon him; he would answer me with total honesty as I was told my child would not survive much longer. I remained at the glass that separated my newborn child from me.

As the reality of mortality began to seek in, I prayed that this child would not experience pain and that if he were to perish that he does so in my arms that I might be with him at that moment he would go to be with God. After notifying the family of our child's condition I noticed my wife beginning to wake. Still in and out of sleep, my wife became restless and upset as she repeated her questions, "How's my baby? How's the baby? Tell me what's going on." I came to her and sat on her bedside. I cradled her head in my hand as I lowered myself to her. I placed a tender kiss upon her cheek and began the task of notification.

Tears began to fall down her face as I softly told her, "It will be okay, please go back to sleep now, sweetheart. I'll be here for you when you wake." I went back to the glass at the isolation room, and what I was about to observe would come to me with overwhelming despair. There was the nurse standing next to this little one. She had no idea I had returned to see her just as she was stroking our baby with one of her fingers up and down his tiny hand ever so gently. This nurse could no longer hold back the tear that rolled down her cheek. Another nurse came into the room and approached the glass, reaching to close the blinds that would separate my child from my view. The nurse standing by our baby turned her head and saw that I had returned. I could read her lips as she whispered one simple word, "No," and the blinds remained opened.

This nurse, holding the hand of my little one, began to stare at me with the compassion of a close friend. Wiping the tear from her cheek, she attempted to provide a small smile in my direction only to return her total attention to her patient, my son. As I looked upon my child, the hours passed and with them so went our child, into the loving arms of God.

Almost thirty years later we still grieve as Sharon and I can visit the gravesite where our child is laid to rest. Within a cemetery in St. Joseph, Missouri, there is a small designated area devoted to small children called Baby Land that serves as a memorial with a statue of a child and a lamb at play. Upon this memorial there is a simple engraving that reads, "God is Love. (Dedicated from the Hoagland Family)."

I have shared the ever-so-short seven hours of Curtis' life in an attempt to reiterate the fact that just like the many parents and friends of children within the oncology wards, there will be parents and friends attending to the needs of other children afflicted with a terminal illness. Regardless of their realization of impending death, when it comes they too will come to know the shock and grief just as we have experienced the loss due to sudden tragedy. Nothing will properly prepare the parents and family members for the loss of a child. Despite the counsel of a physician who explains the impending loss, when it eventually arrives it will always be too soon, and without the preparation they, the parents, once had it will be met with the many emotions that we have all come to know. The forewarning that precedes our loss will not alleviate the strong desire to pay tribute to our child in the way of an everlasting memorial in our child's memory. As I mentioned, there are several memorials that will come in many shapes and forms: a roadside memorial or a private place designated within our homes or property. Just like the many cemeteries throughout the world, there will others who will help finance that new wing at the hospital that cared for their child. The brick walkways that line the hospital entryways are currently being offered to those who wish to donate funds. Once the walkways become complete, a financial need will be fulfilled for the hospital as well as the desired need to have a child or any other loved one remembered, as the bricks are well placed and engraved in honor of lost ones.

Considering Others

Soon after the loss of our child, most will be aware that some type of memorial will be needed and desired. Something that will preserve the memory of the children we once knew in the physical and who now await all of us in the light of God, where we will be reunited with our children and other family members for all eternity in a place free of the pain and the emotions that we endure here on earth.

Memorials

The parents and siblings as well as the other family members and friends will approach one another with their thoughts, wants, and desires as they strive to understand and seek a place and time to honor their loved one. We need to understand and remind ourselves that although we are surviving within our own time frame, recognizing the urgency of others and their personal needs cannot and should not be ignored. The best plan is a well thought out plan. Time will be required to discuss what will best serve the majority while attending to the personal needs of the immediate family most affected by the loss.

In the beginning a well-planned place and time will come to us with such a profound value that we will feel rushed with great vigor to preserve the memories while attempting to dissect the many emotions that plague every waking moment. We need to start with a meeting between the close family members to choose, first, what type of memorial will best serve the requirements of all and what will be an appropriate design that best reflects the child lost. Second, we will schedule a time where all who wish to participate can be present. One or more of these considerations for others may prove to be burdensome at a time in your life filled with the demands of a lifetime. Just remember that your efforts will not go unrewarded. Knowing that considering others as well as yourself will take on a meaning all its own, a time and place for all to remember our loss that will be proven well chosen in the actions and the resolution for each and every one.

Up to this point we have discussed some of the many different types of memorials that will provide comfort for those who desire a lasting tribute for our lost one, a place and time as we consider others. For those residing in acute grief, anything and everything can be related to our child, brother, or sister. Walking past the bedroom that our loved one once occupied, the smells that surround us, their perfume, cologne, even the clothing once warn by them will bring us to uncontrollable tears as our emotions take us from one place in time to another. The triggers that we encounter may unnecessarily extend the normal progress of healing and moving along productively. We may find ourselves preparing weeks and days in advance for the many anniversaries associated with our loved ones. On their birthday, for example, we may recall the birthdays past never to return with the same joyful memories we used to look forward to: the celebration and the presence of them once in the physical, which now will be in the spiritual. We will attempt to prepare for the sadness that we know all too well as the depression is revisited in the acute on the anniversary of their death, first month by month. We know in our hearts that as time passes the monthly reminders will be replaced by the years ahead rather than the days and months we know early on after our loss. Holidays will have new meaning, to say the least. During acute grief we will develop a persona to conceal the sadness in an attempt to spare and not influence others in their time of joy and relevance.

I recall a conversation I had with my oldest son. He said that it recently came upon him as he raised the question what to do about his younger brother's birthday. He told me that he chose not to ignore his brother's birthday as if it had little or no meaning anymore. My son was attempting to resolve his dilemma with concern for others. I knew he would not allow this birthday and the others that would follow to pass without notice. This is when I shared with him that memorials do come in many shapes and forms. Recognizing his brother's birthday could be a healthy day set aside where he could organize the event, inviting his brother's family and closest friends to a predestinated location. If approached within a proper format within an atmosphere to accommodate everyone interested, this day would be designed as a celebration of his brother's life not his death. It is with this thought in mind that I will recommend we attempt to readjust the unwanted schedule, recalling the anniversaries month by month by using a calendar on which we may write the upcoming events as well as the many anniversaries that surround the life of your child. I happen to know firsthand that as time begins its healing process this calendar will take on a new, less burdensome appearance. Take your time, go slowly.

Take Your Time, Go Slowly

Christ and the Little Children

CHAPTER SIX

FAITH

I ask, my friends, regardless of your faith or the lack thereof, that you allow me the privilege of my own belief. My interpretation of faith is a reasonable individual with the God-given gift that is given to all: a mind to reason with, to help us all sort and help us come to some reasonable understanding.

A building constructed on sand will surely crumble and fall. It is only with a strong foundation under the building that we can be comfortable with ourselves that the structure will endure the elements, manmade and those of nature. So it is also true for those of faith. The belief in a supreme being is something that is not innate in us; it is, however, a discipline that we acquire through example or learning, a path we walk, a tool. For those of us with faith, the path less traveled after the loss of our child will be somewhat less troublesome, and somehow we will find comfort that those without faith will lack. That is not to say that a person with faith will not find their faith being tested to the extreme after such a life-changing event. We will question our beliefs as we ponder the big question that can consume us without reasonable understanding: the question of why.

It is my intention to continue down this path of realism with you, and I ask regardless of your faith, whether it be Catholic, Baptist, Pentecostal, or Jewish, or should you be agnostic or atheist, that you continue to read on with an open mind and heart.

FREE WILL

Let us begin by constructing a solid foundation on which to build a mutual understanding of what we do know about God. That is that God is all-understanding, all-loving, all-forgiving, all-knowing, and all-merciful. That God wishes no harm to His beloved children, and that we were made in God's image. If we can agree on this most important belief of what we know God is then the rest of my writing on faith will be easily digested and clearly understood. I have to ask you now that should you be angry with God at this time I understand, and, more important, God understands. But we have to put this emotion back into your basket of emotions for the time being, allowing yourself to approach what I am about to write with an open mind and an open heart. First know that it's okay to be angry with God. He is after all, as we agreed, all understanding, right? For the moment let me say that I know that when you cry, God cries with you. I will explain later in detail just how I know this to be true, and with God's guidance I pray that writing to you on faith is with His approval and to your satisfaction.

Understanding free will vs. predisposition has always been an argument with compelling testimony on both sides, which cannot be ignored. First, predisposition implies, in its simplest example, that a person raised in a controlled environment such as poverty with few or no resources cannot be expected to escape his or her environment without positive intervention. That is not to say that all high-risk individuals are restricted to the low-income housing developments of Chicago, Los Angeles, the Bronx, or any other afflicted area throughout this country. High-risk individuals are also identified in the well-to-do, prolific suburbs of great stature. These may be considered predisposed due to being products of their environment on every spectrum, in or out of poverty, some due to severe family dysfunction or peer pressure and others due to the daily challenge of finding a meal after not eating for several days. As a young child there may have little or nothing at all at their disposal to correct such difficultly, and they may witness the undeniable example of a next-door neighbor or the father of a friend or maybe even the child's own family member profiting by the unopposed sale of drugs or other illicit activities. They will observe the obvious financial benefits that generate regular meals, nice clothing, and that new vehicle as a symbol of confidence and success. Knowing that the activity is illegal seems unimportant next to survival in a world filled with the cruelty of predisposition. For those of predisposed thinking, they contend that there is little or no hope without a strong intervention and that these individuals lack the luxury of free will to change there predestinated outcome.

For the children stuck in the environment I've just described, I can support the "product of our environment theory." I can sympathize, understand, and worry that these children are in danger. But when I have to consider the adult with the mature mind that God has given to all, I find myself in conflict and unsympathetic, knowing that as mature individuals with healthy minds and having the knowledge of right and wrong, we're not the children of days gone past and we do have choices to make to better ourselves and provide a wholesome environment for our families and our future generations to follow.

We have a choice, my friends, and the free will to decide for ourselves when we reach the fork in the road which path to travel. This is free will. If God wanted every one of his children to be the same in every respect without the freedom of choosing for us, life would be without challenge, without conquest or opportunity. Everyone would be the same. But to understand God as a reasonable person, we have to recognize that there are some things God can't do.

What God Can't Do

What God can't do, what our God chooses not to do, or even what our God refuses to do—I cannot play semantics here. I have been well advised that some who read, "What God can't do," may take offense at the knowledge. As you read on, you will discover my own reasonable understanding that is shared by millions worldwide. While I share my beliefs, I can only ask that any reader not take offense with the title of this subchapter. Just replace it with what you personally find comfortable.

Remember that God is all-loving, -caring, and -understanding. Can anyone tell me with any reasonable conviction that such a God that I have come to know and love with all my heart, the Supreme Being, the creator of all life, could or would allow the terrible catastrophic disasters that plague our everyday existence? I think not. Not the God I have come to know, understand, and love. This merciful God would not permit child suffering, poverty, plagues that continue to consume entire populations, sexual abuse, brutal murders, senseless killings, and beheadings in God's own name for his sake. No, my friends, again, I think not. Such distortions are without reasoning. For those of us who have lost a child, this hits home in a very up close and personal way that any other reader may not fully come to appreciate.

We find ourselves asking that undeniable question over and over: why? How can a young child free from sin lie in a hospital bed stricken with leukemia or some other form of illness that will soon take this most precious gift before life has had a chance to begin, life's dreams unfulfilled and so many questions left unanswered? There are so many examples we could share that would mirror this one, and I am sure that after your loss you won't have to look very far. These unanswered questions without a realistic view of what God can and can't do may leave you angry with God without the understanding that God does care about his children. If He could rid your child of his or her terrible fate He would, but we need to accept the fact that God could not. Again, if our merciful God could He would. Know this, my dear friends, that there are things God can do. He can and does answer our prayers. And He knows and feels our great pain, and as we cry in such terrible grief God cries with us. He will wrap his loving arms around you and try to comfort you in this your greatest time of need. God grieves with and for you as He does me and mine.

Allow me to reinforce the above by reminding you that there are bad people on this earth who continue to prosper and flourish by the evilness they bestow upon our society with total disregard and malice towards the victims they lure. The minority that I speak of may have little or no concern for others they knowingly destroy. Consider the drug dealer of the day; I am not referring to the six- to sixteen-year-olds standing on the street corner selling from a concealed pocket. The animal that I refer to is the kingpin that has protected himself by establishing a community that will surround him at the expense of all others. Lives will be lost and countless damages done to families who were at one time healthy with promise and a future. This individual can relax undetected by authorities, knowing his risk factor is minimal at best. He will reap his financial goals while others far down the food chain will face destruction through arrest, overdose, mental illness, or suicide. This kingpin could care less about the lives he will destroy. He will obtain the three-million-dollar house, that new yacht, the most expensive automobiles. He will employ housekeepers to ease the burden for his wife. He will prosper in ways we can only dream about, providing and buying an education for his children while we scrimp and save only to find ourselves in financial ruin.

No one said life was fair, and I don't think it's meant to be. It's free will, my friends, not predisposition. Words such as pride, integrity, morals, and honor will have no real significance for the individual I've just described and yet while on his death bed he may have the opportunity to beg God for forgiveness for his sins against humanity, and our faith teaches us that it shall be given unto him. We may find ourselves asking the question, where's the justice in that, after we have toiled so, enduring hardship after hardship to provide for our families and to keep them as safe as possible from the evil people I have just described? There are many other examples we all could share, I know. I have chosen the kingpin because I believe this to be the catalyst due to its mutation that threatens the future of our society as we have known it in the past. This has to be the utmost on my attention scale, second only to the increasing divorce rate in this country these days. "For better or worse" has taken a backseat recently to the thought that if this marriage fails, I'll just get a divorce and move on. For those that after exhausted all avenues and maintain their marriages remain in crisis, we have to understand that not all marriages are made in heaven and may be irreconcilable, and divorce the only rescue. This will only become more complicated should children be involved. Being raised in a single-parent household is something only a family in such an environment can appreciate. Again, there are some things God can't do. If God could, do you believe that such injustices would be tolerated?

It is not my intention to have you questioning your faith; quite the contrary, it is my intention to help you reinforce your faith in God with an understanding of reasonable thought.

Now that we have built a solid foundation on which to construct, let us begin the task of construction by carefully placing the building blocks, the bricks, or the sticks of our building. These will guide us on the lifelong journey filled with grief and the faith to help us understand, if only to make some degree of reasonable sense of it all. Thereafter, we know we will be on the road to a healthier human being spiritually, physically and mentally.

Assuming we have established a common understanding of what God is, let us move on now and start placing this thought together in our personal lives in relation to what we had and what we have lost. Our circumstances may differ and the ages of our lost children will be different, but what will be a constant are the undeniable loss and the struggle we share and will continue to share in the remaining years of our lives. I'll start by describing my own sons, the eldest still with us and the other two that have passed.

Curtis drew his last breath seven hours after his birth, as I looked upon the infant behind the glass of a private area sheltered from the population in the nursery. The doctor who discussed my baby's condition shortly before the baby's death approached me. The doctor explained that Curtis suffered from an undeveloped kidney, and as a result this led to other complications during the pregnancy and the child would not survive. Curtis, our second child born in 1978, was never awarded the comfort of nurturing parents, and my wife and I felt robbed of the honor of knowing and growing with our child. This, now twenty-seven years later, we still grieve, but I can testify that with time things do get better.

Our third son was taken from us twenty-two days after his twenty-fourth birthday. A kinder, more compassionate human being you'll never meet. Everyone who met him loved him. He filled our lives with love, joy, and great pride. He was a good human being. I would like to write so much more about him, but somehow I think you already know him, don't you? You need not look far, my friends, or you would not be reading this book. My heart goes out to you and yours.

I believe that God knows the children we have lost and that God loves our children unconditionally. Believing this and knowing what "God is" and "what God can't do" does give me comfort, for without my belief, at least for me, I might have strong difficulties with my religious convictions. That is to say, how can a loving, caring, and compassionate God allow the evil people in this world to flourish and prosper and at the same time allow the kind and faithful to suffer a tragic and sudden death without dreams fulfilled?

I have some very dear friends I have come to know and admire and truly respect as God-fearing Christian people with strong beliefs that differ greatly from my own. I respect their beliefs and convictions but it saddens me that they cannot respect mine or even try to understand with an open mind. What they would like me to believe is that God has this great plan of predisposal and that our entire life is somehow well planned in God's scheme of things without understanding. I call it blind faith (eyes wide shut). This train of thought, as it was presented to me, was that I should accept their biblical theory that God had taken my children in some divine plan and that it is not for the parents to question but to accept without question, knowing that at someday in the future the plan would be revealed to us and it would all make sense. Why do some people cling so strongly to their beliefs that they become blind to the beliefs of others? We have the same mind to reason with, the same ability and opportunity to understand with an open mind. As I mentioned, blind faith.

I no more want my writing to overly influence your own beliefs than I want the writing of others who have an abstract view to influence your faith. It has been and will continue to be my desire to give you the opportunity to open that God-given gift of yours, your mind and heart. Consider the evil and the good in the world. Contrast that with a realistic mind, a tool given to you by God Himself to do with what you will. It's called "free will."

What God Can Do

The hardest concepts to convey have passed and hopefully we're still on the same page. If not, that's okay too. Let us continue with the same basic foundation that we started with, that we know who God is. Remember, God is all-understanding, all-loving, all-forgiving, all-knowing, and all-merciful.

The gift of understanding is a blessing from God. All we need do is look around us with an open heart, see the sky, the vast wonders of the world and universe, and understand, just as today's evolutionary theorists and scientists have themselves evolved beyond Darwin's theory of evolution, simply that life is too complicated and the universe too infinite to be discarded by some forethought that man was created from some earth-born metabolic enigma or parasite and not without the intervention of a supreme being.

I have had the privilege of speaking with many scientists during my academic learning who have reinforced the recent age of new thinking that the scientists of the day are more willing to accept the reasonable thought that however man and the great wonders of the universe came to be, they could not have been possible without some divine intervention. That is to say that, by whatever means God chosen at His will to create, the "big bang" or through evolution, God's work is at hand. This has never been as cloquently articulated as it was when I received it from a professor at a college located in a southwest suburb of Chicago. There Mr. Taylor taught several subjects related to science, but the one I enjoyed the most was the class he thought on cosmos, "the maniacal universe." Of all the educators I've encountered throughout my academic endeavors, I am the proud recipient of this man's kind ways. He's a man with a unique sense of humor, a man of strong conviction that is strong to detect at his every entrance, in person or memory. Like me, Professor Taylor asked one thing: that we listen with an attentive ear and an open mind. We developed a close friendship throughout the past fifteen years now and will continue to do so forever. He and his wife, Mrs. Taylor, are true blessings from God. Thank you both.

Blessings from God come to us in many ways. These are the things God "can" do. We may not always recognize a blessing, be it as simple as the tree that grows in your backyard, that blade of grass, or the birds that fly so effortlessly overhead, but they're with us all the same and we will take them for granted. Still there are many other blessings that we receive through prayer. We can pray to God and he will answer, not always the way we may understand or dream about,

Faith

but the prayers will not be ignored. My wife and I recently viewed a movie entitled *Bruce Almighty*, starring Jim Carrey and Morgan Freeman, who accepted the task of playing God for a short time. I have to admit I've never been a great fan of Jim Carrey, although my sons were and are. Nevertheless, Sharon and I did watch and enjoy the plot. I'll spare you the details of this fiction and at the same time recommend it should you find yourself in Blockbuster or the like undecided on a rental.

Shortly after the movie begins, Carrey is given all the powers of God with a strong caution that one of the two rules not to be broken is that of "free will." At this I became interested in a movie that just moments earlier I had predisposed myself not to enjoy. Then soon after, in this movie another bell rang when Carrey became tormented by the subconscious voices in his mind that he soon became aware were neglected prayers left unanswered. Carrey arrives at his solution to the problem by the use of e-mail, and he types, "Answer all prayers, yes," and with the click of a tab on the keyboard everyone receives whatever they had prayed for. Many won the lottery only to discover they were one of thousands to split the jackpot, which became minimal and they became angry with God. Others still received answered prayers in the affirmative and they too became angry and unfulfilled. Carrey then, after total chaos, begs God for help and guidance. God appears to Carrey unsympathetically and allows Carrey his only defense: "I was just trying to make everyone happy. Give them what—" to which God replied, "Since when do my children know what they want?"

This was only a movie and not taken from the Holy Bible. We, all of us, are only human and at times we may not know what's best for us; we know it's wrong of us to play God, to tamper with the free will of others, and so I will not tamper with yours and I will not allow others to play with mine. Keep your faith wherever you find comfort; I would no more impose my beliefs on you than I would allow yours into my comfort zone. I simply ask that, as I have requested in the beginning, you accept with an open mind and an open heart a reasonable explanation of what our God can and cannot do then apply it in your faith and draw a better understanding that it was not God that took our children from us. God would not allow such devastation and the pain that you and I have come to know so acutely. What God has promised us is that He will be there for us, always and forever. God knows you, my friends, better than you know yourself. God can and does answer our prayers. We can pray that God helps us through this, the worst of times on earth, and that He gives the strength in faith and courage to emerge in time with the promise that we will survive this difficult road ahead with his strength. We can pray for God to walk with us along this path filled with grief and sadness knowing, my dear friends, that the greatest gift of all and possibly the hardest to accept after the loss of a child due to a tragic and sudden death without time to say good-bye, is the fact that our prayer will be answered. Please know God will walk that path with you. Just ask Him, He's there. The things God can do.

Within this chapter I must highly recommend a book written by Harold S. Kushner entitled *When Bad Things Happen To Good People,* recently reprinted by Random House Inc. from its original version by Schocken Books Inc. in 1981. A national best-seller then and now. Rabbi Kushner reinforces my beliefs and faith that first came to open my mind and heart as I entered the military during the Vietnam War.

I hope I have not, but should I have failed you within this chapter on faith, Kushner will not.

Whether you hold your faith as it was given to Moses within the old law, like our brothers in Judaism, or that found in the new law, the New Testament, with the birth, life, and death of Jesus Christ, all will encounter the variations and sometimes conflicting interpretations found within the Holy Bible by the several different congregations throughout this world. Each will proclaim their own doctrine with perfusions of faith that all will hold dear to their hearts and souls.

Christianity

I remember back when I was in my childhood years I first became aware of strong faith within the Baptist church. There I came to know a wonderful pastor named Bill Mills. I recall the kindness within Bill's heart and soul as he entered the children's Bible study group, accompanied by my younger brothers, that was located in the basement area of the church. This soft-spoken young man approached the fifteen or so students with open arms and a smile that I can best describe as one of compassion and understanding. After introducing himself as a Bible study teacher within the church, he distributed handouts to all the children along with some simple homework assignments to be returned the next week. One of the assignments was that we prepare ourselves to accept Jesus Christ as our personal savior; in doing so we were instructed to memorize a passage found within the book of John, the most important doctrine of the Baptist faith. We were told we would openly profess our union with God. It reads:

"For God so loved the world, that he gave his only begotten son,
That whosoever believeth in him should not perish,
But have everlasting life."

John 3:16

For those of us in Christianity, John 3:16 will forever remain within our long-term memories with great pleasure, as we now in adulthood will teach our own children.

Regardless of faith, we need to understand that God's gifts (blessings) are so abundant we will not always recognize all of them with complete appreciation, while others will be profound with true understanding acknowledging God's presence within our hearts, minds, and souls. Each and every time, these blessings will fill us with the enhancement of faith renewed.

Soon after Sharon and I were married in 1974, we began to accept the fact that if we were to raise our children properly we needed to expand our education in the many different faiths. We felt a personal responsibility to each other as soul mates as well as the strong desire to welcome our children who would soon arrive into a Christian family. In our ten years of searching for just the right place of worship we traveled extensively, visiting many churches in which we felt comfortable and some that did not. We discovered faiths that spoke in tongues where the congregation worked themselves up into a profuse sweat as they jumped from their seats screaming at the top of their lungs and gave thanks to the Lord, Bible in hand, dancing within the aisles, knocking over chairs, and interrupting the message of God.

Still there were others that we have considered to be Bible thumpers in the extreme. First asked to identify ourselves as visitors, the congregation would welcome us with applause. Later Sharon and I found ourselves startled and alarmed when we were approached by parishioners waiving a Bible inches from our faces as they loudly instructed us to kneel, right there and then, to beg God's forgiveness for being ungrateful sinners in the eyes of God. We, Sharon and I, found ourselves actually fearful to get up and leave, fearing that one of these parishioners would see us bailing out and come running to strike us down, condemning us for all time as they spoke their interpersonal interpretation of the word of God. It would be a long time before we would ever identify ourselves as visitors again.

Let me remind you of what I had written earlier, at the beginning of this chapter on faith; that it is not my intention to encumber, to challenge, or to intrude upon your faith as you receive it within your personal comfort zone, and I would hope that this statement is mutual. As Sharon and I continued our search we visited several other places of worship where we found the word of God well received by others as well as yourselves. Then, after several years we reminded ourselves that we must take personal responsibility for ourselves as well as the needs of our children as we deemed proper and fit. Just as you did, so did we. She and I had to go where we personally found God.

For us we found it in Catholicism, with the tradition that enriched our hearts and souls. Here we discovered one of the greatest gifts of understanding that is shared by those within the parishes worldwide: that there are many paths to God, and while we as Catholics will adhere to our doctrine through the profession of faith, we are not to judge others within their religious communities, for it is said that "where even two shall gather and pray in the light of God, there too he shall be."

I have learned early in life that there are two subjects on earth that may end friendships with strong debate. The first will be politics and the second is found within one's personal choice of faith or that of religion. I find myself unable to separate the two, as I have to

Faith

believe you cannot be a strong leader without the benefit of faith to guide you, lead you. Those elected into office will find themselves approached with controversy having to make the difficult decisions that will affect all, not just the one. A simple example of the union found in faith and politics is in our hands almost every day. When was the last time you read the back of any United States currency? Remember? "In God We Trust." This currency has been held in the highest regard worldwide for generations. If you think I am getting a little off track here, read what Father Bob wrote as it appeared in a recent newsletter at a local parish in central Florida. With Father Bob's kind permission I copy:

Dear Brothers and Sisters,

The good news is that the presidential election is almost here and we will not be subjected to all those awful ads—the bad news is that whoever is elected will not be the savior he claims to be. High expectations … but the reality is less so. Only in Christ Jesus are the poor heard and the powerless given real attention.

In the sacred Scriptures we are told of a God who does justice. A God who is merciful and forgiving, a God who seeks the good of his people. In Jesus we have a savior who includes all people, who does not turn from the lame, the halt, and the blind. In Jesus we have one who is willing to lay His life on the line. Jesus the innocent accepts death, death on the cross to grant us salvation. Salvation is a free gift. There are no strings attached. Believe and be saved. Jesus' offer is not empty or self-serving. Our God desires that we live in

God's kingdom forever. God wishes the salvation of the sinner. We can trust in God and the absolute love that Jesus shows us. The Scriptures constantly remind us that God calls us, as we are, no show, no pretense. The promise is beyond our expectations. John the Evangelist says that what we are now is God's children, what we are to be is beyond anything we can imagine. (John 3:16).

My dear friends, all I ask is that you open your minds and hearts, and as you pray ask God for understanding and guidance. It is written,

"Come unto me, all ye that labour, and are heavy laden, and I will give you rest; Take my yoke upon you, and learn of me: for I am meek and lowly in heart; and ye shall find unto your souls; For my yoke is easy, and my burden light."
St. Matthew 11:28-30

I know that in the beginning after the loss of a child, God's blessings may be difficult to recognize and understand. But I tell you now within reflection as it first came to me in 1978, it may seem a lifetime, but please find some comfort, however little it may come to you now, that acceptance through faith will bring peace, still knowing that our lives have changed forever. In time it will become less burdensome. Know as well that although it may seem alien to you now, you began the journey into healing the moment you left

Faith

shock. Know further that you are not alone on your journey, that God walks beside you, helping you, his kind and wonderful hand resting upon your shoulder as you walk along this road less traveled.

God bless you, my dear friends, one and all.

༃ CHAPTER SEVEN ༄

OTHER FAMILY MEMBERS AND FRIENDS

I feel that it would not be in the best interest of any family member, parent, or mature sibling not to recognize our extended families and loving friends, as they too will struggle after the loss of our child. They will find themselves on their own road less traveled through the grieving cycle with their own triggers that will place them on that roller-coaster ride filled with a majority of the same emotions that we as parents and siblings have come to know. And for some, their lives will also be changed forever depending on the relationships they developed with our child.

For the many who will cherish the loving memories of our child, they will now find themselves forced into the reality we have all come to share, that such a loss, only once aware of in many unknown families, has now become acutely recognized in our lives with the true understanding of mortality.

At times we may find ourselves challenged as we become aware of the fact that some of our relationships, and those of our children, family, and friends, will not recognize our loss. Some may be totally indifferent and lack the sensitivity associated with their own set of priorities and dispositions, free of the emotions that have affected so many around us. It will be easier to understand that some friendships will appear to be unaffected by the news of our loss due to their lack of understanding on this road less traveled; it will, however, become unsettling for us when a family member who we thought had a close relationship with our child approaches us without feelings and empathic qualities and that will take us off guard. This scenario is mentioned only to better illustrate the heartfelt realization that there may be others close to us and our child lost who will not be aware of our full awareness and perception, we may have misjudged the relationship of those who will not acknowledge this catastrophe without sympathy and some understanding. Your basket runneth over with emotions, my friends. Please do not allow this disappointment in others to intrude upon you; rather, attempt to understand that while for us parents and siblings who strive to keep the joyful memories alive in ourselves and other loving family members and friends, these unaffected individuals will be a minority in our lives and will not reflect the true understanding that the others in our lives will share.

Loving Relationships

Without losing focus on the main objective of this book, for the parents and siblings and the loss of a child with no time to say goodbye, there are others who played an intricate and meaningful role in the life of our child that we cannot ignore.

Consider the grandparents, aunts, uncles, cousins, and our child's friendships as well as our own close friends. For those mentioned, some have enjoyed the close relationships they cultivated as caregivers and mentors. Some have made themselves available for our child, who may have sought advice due to an open-door policy with open arms and warm hearts, often reinforced with words of wisdom and confidence. These loving family members and mentors took the time when needed as they were called upon from our child and accepted the challenge with pride and the opportunity to provide sound advice and guidance, not because they may have been asked, but because they chose to.

For a grandparent who had the opportunity will rejoice with great elation at the birth of our children, bringing back the vivid memories of their own child-rearing days long past. It will seem like yesterday when the grandparents began writing in the book filled with blank pages, which the grandparents managed to fill with writings of their own experiences, their trials and errors, the raising of children, and with an abundance of love and nurturing. The correlation between raising their own children and raising a grandchild may be strong and healthy, second only to raising their own children. The relationship could be as strong as that of a parent; they too will enjoy the privilege of observing the grandchild mature with the same heartfelt pride that we as parents have come to know.

A grandparent with such a relationship as I've just described will not elude the emotions that we parents are experiencing, that basket of emotions recently dropped onto our laps; again, the same may be true for so many aunts, uncles, and close friends. After receiving notification of the tragic and sudden death of a grandchild, a grandparent may find themselves overcome with the shock that will change their lives forever, filled with overwhelming grief so much like our own.

In the subchapter on grief I simply touched on the many "triggers" that will send us like a slingshot back into moments of despair. A grandmother speaks of her grandchild that was taken from the family and from her personally, from her own life. Her grandson was killed while taking a short walk to see a friend. Soon after the child began walking it began to rain. The grandchild found himself in a downpour at the same time a young, inattentive driver struck her grandchild from behind, claiming the grandchild's life instantly:

I try and remember all the happy times we shared, his wonderful personality, his smiling face, and the immeasurable joy he gifted me. I have several grandchildren and even a few great-grandchildren, but the relationship I had with this grandchild was unique in that he often would walk into my life at the turn of a doorknob unannounced, come to me with a well-placed kiss upon my cheek, for which he was so well known, and ask, "What's up, Grandma?" He would sit close to me and we would talk about anything that was on his mind. We would laugh together, enjoying each other's company as we passed the time being together. He had a wonderful relationship with his mother and father, but as with all children they may feel a need to discuss a thought or a problem with someone they trusted. He knew he could depend on me as an alternative, or maybe as a second opinion to reinforce his decision-making. I will remember him as a gentle, loving, caring, and kind young man that left us all. I have my moments that bring me to tears with extreme sadness that I am sure will plague me the remaining years of my life. I once enjoyed the rain showers that would come and go and the sweet smell that lingered long after the rain would end. Now when it rains I find myself overcome with the sadness, remembering my grandson's last moments on earth. Still to this day, at times when I least expect it, the door will open and for a fleeting moment in time I may look up for my grandson, smiling as he walks through that doorway and back into my life.

Such a loving and caring relationship will not be left out in the rain of sadness. Much like the parents and siblings, this grandmother had cultivated her relationship and as time continues she will reap the harvest of joyful memories that will replace her sadness with the moments of a job well done. Never having to be asked, she gladly accepted the task and responsibility; and maybe that's why we call these mothers grand.

I remember an occasion a few years past, having a conversation with a co-worker, a college and cherished friend. I may have just been venting but what I needed was advice. As we sat having a cup of coffee, I began by explaining some difficulties my son was experiencing as he struggled through an intense period of his adolescence. My dear friend Mike provided what I needed most: first, an attentive ear and later a large, very large hand upon my shoulder, followed by reinforcing advice. Mike is one of those people that would stand out in a crowd. Without knowing the gentle kindness that filled his heart, Mike has an appearance that often intimidated others around him at his very presence, though he did nothing or spoke in any manner that would warrant his unwanted attention. However, Mike would not be a man to wrong; if need be, Mike was more than capable of correcting mistakes directed at him personally or those directed towards his family. I had no idea upon my first introduction to this man that Mike and his family would later become such valued members of my family. Having the privilege and the trust in knowing Mike I would soon welcome his kind offer to become involved and to counsel my son in need, with the promise of providing the unobtrusive attention. So without delay Mike made a phone call to my son and instructed him to the back door of my home, where Mike would arrive and pick up my child for a drive that later provided a reasonable explanation that would ease my son's concerns. What they spoke of still remains a mystery to me. It must have been something they chose to keep in confidence.

I chose this story at this time to illustrate to you that friendships often develop into strong relationships that will last for years to come and that Mike was a tool, a blessing that evolved beyond that of just one son and extended onto the younger brother as they too developed a relationship that would later break Big Mike's heart. Mike and I had made a strong correlation with our children. Mike has three children, similar in age to my two boys. For Mike and me, it was not just his children and mine; we had developed extended families as we observed them grow and mature with the joy and pride felt by a parent's accomplishment.

When word of my son's tragic and sudden death reached Mike, he was one of the first to call. I remember Mike's kind conversation; his shock at our loss was devastating. He was filled with tears and overwhelming sadness. Later I would be reminded that Mike had lost someone that meant very much to him, as if it were one of his own.

Soon after the news of a child's death reaches the ears of others, especially family and close friends, there will be knocks at our doors and the telephone will ring with frequency. Condolences will be abundant from those who will reach out to you the only way they know how. They too will find themselves in their own state of shock filled with the memories of our children lost. They will be driven by concern not just for our child but also for you, the parents and siblings. These loving, caring friends will arrive with open arms and a tear in their eye, with the best intentions and strong desire to rush to your aid. They to will be forced to take a step back cognitively as they have been visited by any parent's worst nightmare. A new sense of self-realization will take on a new form, as they will become unwelcome recipients as they discover a new understanding of mortality. Such was the case one Sunday in May 2004 when two loving friends arrived at my doorstep. This story you're about to read will have a familiar ring to it, which I'm sure all will make reference to as we continue to explore family members and loving friends.

I will never forget this day as long as I live. I have to be honest with you that even though their visit was pre-arranged and well planned in advance, my wife Sharon and I were still in acute grief and felt we were not yet ready for any social interaction. We agreed to the visit that I would later recognize as a gift, knowing that I would never trade that wonderful, loving visit filled with kindness and consoling. They arrived with the reinforcing gift of their strong faith, which they provided freely with the best intentions. Although our beliefs may differ as to who and what God's is, I respect their interpretation that they share with the millions of our brothers and sisters within the Baptist faith. As the doorbell rang, I took a deep breath and opened the door to great our friends, Greg and his wife,

Norma. I looked into Greg's eyes. I saw the sadness and concern that seemed to emanate from the both of them. I felt that lump return to my throat accompanied by blurred vision. As we greeted each other, Greg swiftly came to me with open arms and a strong embrace as he asked, "Buddy, how are you? I've missed you so," and right behind Greg came his loving wife, Norma, to relay the same sentiment. What just moments earlier felt intrusive now became an overwhelming welcome of joy. As I looked on they went to Sharon with the same loving embraces, and what was temporarily lost returned to Sharon with a faint smile that filled my heart and soul with relief and some disappointment within myself.

Up to this point I had neglected one of the most important needs during the grieving process: the gift of extended family relationships. Not only had I temporality forgotten the need of my wife but I had also ignored the needs of others such as Greg and Norma. You see, my friend Greg and I were not only co-workers; we were then and remain to be brothers in Christ. Just as Greg embraced my children, I too enjoyed the privilege of our close relationship as I came to know Greg's immediate family, his soul mate Norma, and their children, Debbie, Lisa, and their youngest, Jonathan. Within the law enforcement community we who have been called to serve soon recognize that the children of police officers develop in one of two ways. They may become problematic in defiance as they enter into the difficult stages of adolescence. Some may struggle in their personal lives, attempting to gain independence and identification, while the others may move along totally unaware and become productive members of our society; in either case, the majority of our children will emerge from the difficult trials of adolescence and choosing their own way in this world to be whatever they wish to be. Some may strive to follow in their father or mother's footsteps. The latter was true for Jon, as it was for my sons. Both Jonathan and my youngest son joined the police cadet program when they turned fifteen. Our son's request to participate in a ride-along would be granted by Greg and me as we saw fit within our own comfort zone.

I recall one evening on the midnight shift, I met with Greg, my supervisor at the time, and told him now that things had calmed downed. I felt it was relatively safe to pick up my youngest son, who was waiting for the opportunity to come out as my partner on patrol. Greg told me that his son Jon was also waiting to join him as well. As so many times in the past, we would take turns making the "pick up." This meant that we would take turns picking up the coffee for ourselves and the soda or hot chocolate for the youngsters. This was during those hours after the dispatches for aid had begun to decrease and as all officers found themselves in boredom. (For those of you without this understanding I will inform you that police work consists of 98 percent boredom and 2 percent sheer panic.) I suppose it was always the same, but on this particular coffee break I remember that evening above all the previous. We met at a pre-designated place, squads parked next to each other, and Greg and

I enjoyed our coffee and the boys, now in their late teens, stood by themselves not far from their fathers, engaged in conversation with laughter and wonderful smiles as they consumed their beverage of choice. By now they have developed a friendship personally as well as within the law enforcement community that Greg and I knew all too well. They were so similar in so many ways, their outgoing personalities that seemed to radiate affection to all they encountered. It has been relayed to me on several occasions that to know these two young men was to love them. Both were well received among other co-workers as Greg and I looked on with overwhelming pride and joy.

I remember this one evening in particular in which, as our children were conversing and Greg and I were talking about God knows what, I became acutely aware of Greg's posture, his huge smile, standing tall, coffee cup in hand. He was gazing upon our sons as they enjoyed each other's company. We were actually watching our children growing up before our eyes, and we were pleased.

Keeping this recollection in mind, let us return to that visit by Greg and Norma some two months after the death of my youngest child, as the uncertain future will soon be revealed.

Soon after Sharon, Norma, Greg, and I returned from church that morning, we began discussing the loss we all shared. We sat comfortably at the dining room table trying to enjoy the lunch Sharon had prepared; we began discussing our children and the significance of our faith. After lunch Greg and I retired to the backyard, leaving our wives in privacy. Despite Greg's excuse to smoke his cigar, I knew what his real intentions were and I did not object. The both of us needed to relive the memories of times past and the future that lies ahead. Sitting in the sunshine in central Florida, Greg said all the right things. He told me that he too felt the sadness of our loss, as we reflected upon the days past filled the wonderful memories that no one could take from us, and that somehow God would see us through this. Greg tried to apologize for not making it to the wake and funeral. I quickly reminded him that during our telephone conversation the day after my son was killed, it was he who said in a very shaky voice, "I'm on the way, Ron, I'll be with you soon," and that it was I who told him not to come; not because I didn't want to see him, but because I was very much aware of the obligations he faced within his church that could not be left on hold. I had to talk him out of making the twelve-hundred-mile trip from Florida to Chicago. I told Greg that we would be okay and that his phone call and his strong desire to be with me was well received. He told me that his son Jonathan was going to be with us, and that this kind young man would represent his entire family.

While in the state of shock, so many hours will pass in a fog, while others will stand out in our minds and hearts. During my son's wake I remember I was standing just a few feet from where my son lay when I felt a hand resting on my right shoulder. I turned there stood Jon, his eyes red and his face filled with sadness and compassion. Jonathan stood by me for quite a while; we were recalling the days that he and my son had spent together and that he was going to miss him very much. He would not leave my side as others would approach me with condolences. Jon told me how honored he was to represent his family and that there wasn't anything that could keep him from attending.

As I told Greg of this experience I also shared with him that as I looked upon this young man I found myself filled with the memories of Jon from a small child to the young man that stood at my side. Like a picture slideshow in slow motion, I felt the strong ties we shared as I treasured every moment, not just because of their friendship, but also as most extended family members will look upon these children as one of our own. I continued to tell Greg that just as Jon had come to me like so many other young people that evening, I felt an overwhelming concern for all of them as I found myself praying to God that he watch over all these young, tender souls. I asked God to protect them from harm.

As I was speaking to Greg I noticed a tear roll down his face with an expression of fear and sadness. Greg pulled his chair closer to mine as he led us in prayer. We prayed for understanding and guidance; we prayed for strength and intervention not just for ourselves but also for the many other families that were currently struggling after losing a child. As we prayed I intervened and asked that God protect all the children in our lives especially Greg and Norma's son Jonathan, who was now employed as a police officer for the city of Joliet, Illinois. I heard the choking in Greg's voice, which raised my attention to the tears streaming down his face. Just as all parents who have lost a child, he too had developed his own sense of our fragile mortality. I began to apologize to Greg. I told him not to pay me any mind; that I was just a little overprotective and anything I said may be taken in the wrong light.

Here we were, two grown men crying like babies. Greg raised his hand as he looked at me and told me that he could not begin to understand how I felt after our loss. He said, "I don't think anyone can truly understand unless they themselves have been there." I remember telling my friend that I would never want anyone to go through what Sharon and I had and then, just as I was telling Greg that if I could, I would take this terrible pain from anyone I encounter without reservation, he reminded me that all life is a gift from God that is not to be taken for granted, to which I agreed wholeheartedly.

A few hours later, the evening came to a close with well wishes and, again, prayer. Sharon and I followed our friends to their car that was parked on our driveway; we watched on as they drove away with the promise that we would be speaking soon. Approximately three months passed, with several phone calls from Greg and Norma calling to check up, to see how we were getting on, and if we needed anything. Such calls received by caring family and friends will provide the comfort that will prove to be helpful as they reach out to all of us with tenderness and love.

Then on the evening of the twentieth of August 2004, as Sharon and I were trying to relax after yet another day filled with the despair within acute grief, the telephone rang. I answered and recognized the voice of another co-worker, Marty, my ex-partner in the detective office. He said, "Ron, I'm sorry to have to call but I know how close you and Greg are and I thought it best I make this call myself. I have some bad news."

I looked on and saw that Sharon was listening attentively. I remember asking, "Oh God, what now?" I felt that innate alarm system within going off full blast. As I relapsed into the beginning stage of shock that we all know too well, Marty made the notification that Greg's son Jonathan had been killed just a few short hours ago while on duty responding to an alarm call when the squad he was driving was T-boned by a hit-and-run driver. I was told that Norma was in the Chicago area and that Marty was unsure as to the whereabouts of Greg.

I remember hanging up the phone as Sharon was asking what's going on. I gave her the news that Jonathan was killed just a few hours ago. As I gave her the details as they were relayed to me, we felt our overwhelming sadness compile. I asked Sharon, when would this ever end? First, the loss of our son and now, eight days shy of five short months, we have lost another child within our law enforcement community. Overcome with emotion I realized that now it was our turn to come to the aid of our extended family, Greg and Norma. As Sharon was pacing, holding her hands to her face filled with tears, we found ourselves removed, back in time, and we were reliving tragedy all over again. I told Sharon we had to go to Greg and Norma without delay. She agreed and began packing for the trip back to Chicago. I telephoned Greg and Norma to see what imminent needs they might require. Norma answered the phone and immediately recognized my voice. She went into uncontrolled tears. Sobbing Norma told me she had her daughters with her and they were awaiting Greg's arrival. I told Norma that Sharon and I would soon be on our way and that as soon as we reached town I would be calling. I told her how sorry we were and that soon we would be with them. She replied with a simple "thank you," and within a few hours we were on our way.

While driving the twelve hundred miles, I become filled with the emotions we all know so very well: the shock, acute grief, and the memories of this child as well as the recent visit just a few short months ago of Greg and Norma. They, unaware during shock, would soon realize they had unwillingly entered into the subculture of parents and siblings left with no time to say good-bye. They had begun their long journey on this road less traveled, as they too would not be spared this life-changing event and the grieving cycle that awaited them. That awaits all of us.

This chapter on recognizing other family members and loving friends I dedicate to the two friends in Christ that have lived on this earth for such a short time but who have contributed much; friends, first on earth and now united with each other in heaven, in the light of our loving God.

℘ CHAPTER EIGHT ☙

HEALING

Before we begin to explore the many different and complicated issues that may encumber our road to healing, we need to remember some of these issues that we have previously considered. First, we must recognize our own timetable and that, despite the well wishes of others, each and every one of us is dealing with our own set of new priorities along with the large array of emotions that we must recognize as we continually labor to dissect and manage the sadness that has filled our basket, and which, if permitted, will continue to consume all of as. Should we fail to address these feelings individually, we may find that our travels to a healthier self could be regressed unnecessarily. The words of encouragement that follow will ease your way with the promise of trust and a future filled with emotions that will soon replace the memories of discomfort with those of happy and joyful recollections and that truly reflect the personality and the wonderful gifts our children have bestowed upon all of us in a most joyful and wonderful way. Hopefully this will aid you and yours as we maneuver along this winding path, physically, mentally, and spiritually.

On the Road

Embarking on this road to healing will be a lifelong event for all. However, it is a journey made with the promise that within our own timetable, as the days, months, and years slowly pass, we will recognize the days spent in acute grief, and so the grief that follows will become less problematic. There will be a place in time where unpleasant dreams will be replaced with memories of joyful reminders that will ease your way along your journey.

I have mentioned at the beginning of chapter one, and it has been spoken of and written many times throughout history, that without knowing where we have been we cannot know where we're going, lest we are destined to repeat history. At times we will have to remind ourselves that, as our lessons in history have taught us, we must strive for a healthier existence. Within our own timetable, during the grieving cycle, there will come a time when we find ourselves leaving our denial behind as we become aware of the fact that life must go on and that we must be a productive part of it.

Healing

Depression-Sadness

Within chapter four we discussed only three of the emotions that I consider to be the most significant after the loss of a child, as well as the effects that these emotions may encumber our personal life in a future without this child. Within the first year or so, we will become overwhelmed as we attempt to dissect the many emotions that have recently been dropped onto our laps. During the stage of acute grief, it is not uncommon for some of us to discover thoughts of suicide entering our awareness. We need to understand that we have entered into a world where few will come, and I don't have to tell you that you're life has changed forever. All of the parents and siblings will experience the strong desire to be with their child lost. Within the early stages of shock including that found in acute grief or Post-Traumatic Stress Disorder (PTSD), some will become unable to sort through their basket of emotions without help from others. The thought of suicide is **not** abnormal, due to the fact that we will long to be with our children lost and a life without our children will seem incomplete and meaningless. During this mindset we will soon become aware of the fact that there are others in our lives that need us just as much as we need them. These contradictions in our lives are complicated and need to be defined, knowing they are free of neuroses or psychosis.

An important and positive part of anger is that anger can alert us to danger. Within our mind a bell may go off that something is not right; we find ourselves alerted to the needs of others as well as ourselves. If we discover that the normal thought of suicide is being replaced by that of planning the means by which we can best achieve the desire of suicide, we must take action immediately and without delay. Our life or that of another can be at risk, a risk that is unnecessary and dangerous at best.

Some of the danger signs will be as easy to see as those heard within conversation, while others will not be as evident; they may be elusive to those of us who are not the trained professionals that are at our disposal. An example of elusiveness can be a statement from a loved one: "I don't know how I'm going to get through this without my child," compared to a statement like, "I cannot go on living in this world without my child anymore." The first can be considered reaching out for some understanding during the normal grieving cycle, and the second seems to imply that a decision has been made or perhaps it is a cry for help in despair. In both cases you will find it necessary to seek that professional who can properly make a diagnosis.

I have to caution you here not to rely on your own instincts; you are well advised to seek help regardless of cooperation. Think positively and **trust that you or a loved one will not always feel like this,** and if you feel treatment is the answer then take the precaution and rest knowing you have done well for yourself or for someone else. I speak intelligently in this area, my friends, having experienced suicidal thoughts on both ends of the spectrum. First

I felt despair after the loss of a newborn, then several years later came the loss of my youngest. After the second loss, I admit to you, my dear friends, that I was one of those who found his survival in question. I did not speak of it with anyone, but I felt as if no one needed me around anymore, and I so wanted to join my son, to be by his side, to hold, to kiss, and love again. If it were not for my loving wife, as well as family members and close friends, I may have been one of the few who found themselves questioning their existence. Their concerns and encouragement were conveyed upon me in such a manner that I agreed to seek help.

After a small period of trial and error, we found a qualified therapist who treated me effectively and almost immediately diagnosed my condition as severe depression (PTSD). After a few short weeks I began to feel better, knowing and recognizing what had eluded me temporarily: the fact that I still had a loving wife at my side and another child who needed my attention as well as the grandchildren that I so dearly cherished.

Some things are uncomfortable to talk about, and the only reason I chose to share my personal affliction with you is—in my continued attempt to speak to you as a parent to a parent, knowing the pain and turmoil that surrounds us daily—to provide support and the encouragement needed to survive into a healthier self; to let you know that you're not alone. I hope and pray I have been successful.

Within this world's industrialized societies these days we will discover many avenues to healing. Most will hopefully seek relief and comfort found in our modern medicine that continues to leap forward with astounding progress; others will experiment within unconventional areas such as fortunetellers that for a price will hold a séance with the promise of communicating with the deceased. Still others will find themselves looking to Eastern healing methods and thoughts. I have learned a long time ago not to question some things I don't understand; however, I consider myself reasonably intelligent and cannot and will not accept some trains of thought that I personally find and consider an intrusion as well as dangerous for all, within my own personal comfort zone. You must do the same without prejudice as you find your needs require attention, and direct your efforts toward what you find at your disposal that will provide the best results for you.

Within the chapter on faith, I recognized the healing qualities of prayer and the belief in God, and defined faith as a reasonable person with the God-given gift of a mind to reason, with relative understanding. I see faith as the strongest influence on earth. There are some individuals out there that may relay solely on faith alone. Those of extremely strong religious convictions may pray to God, asking for God's intervention and that God will bestow upon them the healing powers that we find throughout the Holy Bible. As a realist and a strong advocate of "free will," I have to believe that while God does answer our prayers in so many ways, God has given us free will and expects us to take personal responsibility for ourselves, our minds, and our bodies as well as cultivating our spirituality. Know that God wants us to recover to a healthier self, without rejecting the miracle from Him that can be found within that of modern medicine.

Seeking Help

Throughout this book, I have mentioned several times that for those of us who will experience the human emotions with great magnitude after the loss of our children, we will enter the difficult stages of grief. If left unattended, these stages will unnecessarily intrude upon our road to healing physically, mentally, and spiritually.

Within the beginning stages of grief after our loss, the overwhelming majority of survivors will find that their lives have changed forever. After being confronted by our loss, we will discover that our existence on earth may become compounded by our complicated basket of emotions, which will not only intrude upon our minds and souls but also can be recognized in the body as well. As we evolve through the grieving process, some will become aware that it is beginning to take a toll on our physical bodies. To one degree or another, each and every individual will be affected. Some will discover weight loss or weight gain; still others may find themselves neglecting their appearance, not washing their bodies, nor attending to one's personal grooming. Some may recognize that we are drained of energy, as we may find ourselves in restless sleep and

Take Your Time, Go Slowly

unable to complete the long day without a nap. Completely overcome with despair, the pain first recognized as shock and then through the emotions of the grieving cycle will take on a new measure that can affect our psychical health. We know we will be unable to care for the many others in our lives unless we take care of ourselves.

Again, I strongly express to you that your eminent concerns be directed to that of conventional medicine. Then and only then can we afford to seek help found in other resources at our disposal such as those discovered within mind and body medicine; proper and healthy nutrition; and herbal medicine, such as that found within the medicinal properties of St. John's Wort, which has proved to be effective in dealing with the progressive stages of depression. Others may include unconventional Western therapies such as movement education as well as integrative medicine.[4]

I believe that no one should dismiss any train of thought when seeking help. There is an abundance of healthcare providers out there that specialize in one form or another. I have said several times throughout my life, "Don't question or dismiss things that you don't understand." For me personally, this will hold true for almost every train of thought when we begin seeking the help that some will so desperately require. However, there will be a few that I find myself in total disbelief such as palm readers and the like. Again, please do your homework here and seek the many that have the proper training and intelligence and who can enter your personal comfort zone.

Everyone these days will become aware of the fact that within this complicated world stress will touch all of us to some degree or another. Knowing that stress can be the number-one affliction that intrudes upon our health, psychologically and physically, many will seek help by attending a stress management course in an attempt to relieve this widely misunderstood intrusion. Stress in its moderate form will be discovered first within early childhood as children find themselves uncomfortable with the demands of their parents during potty training or as the children experience what appears to be frustration at play during the cognitive years. Later, stress will become recognized with escalation as we develop through adolescence, early adulthood, middle age, and then into old age.

Stress can be found at school as our children find themselves in conflict due to peer pressure or by cramming for exams; later, stress can be self-imposed within the family structure, personally and or financially, as well as by demands discovered at the workplace. As we progress through our lives, stressors may become intrusive to the point that stress is elevated through the stages found within that of stress management or the inability to maneuver along our road, as demands may manifest in panic attacks or the many symptoms related to depression. Stress will not remain within our psyche but can also become dangerous to our physical bodies, such as through lack of energy, changes in appetite resulting in weight loss or gain, restless sleep, or severe mood swings, just to mention a few. Stress can affect our cardiovascular system, creating irregular heartbeats that if left unattended will over time take their toll on our internal organs, creating permanent damage.

In the beginning stages of grief, stress will hold no value. It is later when we find ourselves emerging from normal grief into healing and discovering the holidays and anniversaries that will soon come upon us that we are sent back and forth much like a ping-pong ball.

All of us know the right things we should be doing to get on our way to a healthier self, such as exercising, forcing oneself out of the house, developing a routine from morning till night, eating regular, healthy meals, and practicing proper hygiene. For most, this advice, which we ourselves have given to others, takes extreme effort within this place where few will come, thank God. Let us remind ourselves that **time will bring with it peace of mind to a more manageable degree.**

After seeking the professional guidance found in that of modern medicine, we can now explore and search out the many self-help or support groups and organizations that have so much to offer. They help us place one foot in front of the other with their kind ways and intelligent instruction. Such was the case for my eldest son and me as we enrolled and participated at a stress management workshop offered through Governors State University located in University Park, Illinois.

This class entitled Relaxing Works Wonders proved to be a tool that my son and I can and will reflect upon often with little effort, remembering a very kind and intelligent lady named Paula. Upon our arrival we (my son and I) entered the building and soon found the room designated for the class. We entered the classroom and were set back a step as this petite lady raised her head acknowledging our entrance. She approached us with her introduction, hand extended, welcoming us with attentive eyes and a warm smile. Believe me, my friends, this is not always the case with other instructors. After her introduction she asked us to find a comfortable place to sit; the class (retreat) would soon begin. As Paula addressed the class and introduced the course, she immediately had our undivided attention. It was the way in which she approached the class with her enthusiasm and true conviction. A sense of calm emanated from her very presence.

As Paula described the course, she asked us to give ourselves a break and said that human beings are not built to sit at a desk for hours at a stretch—that's why breaks were invented. She continued to explain that there are simple techniques that rejuvenate the body, mind, and spirit so we can return to our ventures refreshed and ready to accomplish great things. Paula explained that she would teach us how to awaken the senses, take breaks without breaking, practice skill builders, and energize ourselves with physical movements. She instructed the class on proper breathing, sleeping, nutrition, and interpersonal centering within the mind, body, and soul. Paula explained some of the many benefits derived from the teaching found within that of the Eastern tradition known as Qigong and its many forms including Tai Chi. Paula believes that they are, at their least, incredible healing tools that you can use right away at no cost to rehabilitate your health. They literally regenerate temporarily deficient and exhausted tissues, glands, and organs. At their greatest, they are the seed skills for enhanced mental and physical capability and they are the foundation tools for spiritual growth.

Within Paula's class she introduced the strong significance we may find in music. She drew our attention to the writing of Don Campbell: "You know that music can affect your mood? It can make you happy, enchanted, inspired, wistful, excited, empowered, comforted, and heroic." Don Campbell believes and writes, "Music is good for you, physically, emotionally, and spiritually, that the dramatic accounts of how doctors, shamans, musicians, and healthcare professionals use music to deal with everything from anxiety to cancer, high blood pressure, chronic pain, dyslexia, as well as mental illness." For more on this subject, please read Don Campbell's book *The Mozart Effect*.[5]

The well-known group Alabama performs the following example:

Angels Among Us

I was walking home from school on a cold winter day.
Took a shortcut through the woods, and I lost my way.
It was getting late, and I was scared and alone.
But then a kind old man took my hand and led me home.
Mama couldn't see him, but he was standing there,
And I knew in my heart he was the answer to my prayers.

Healing

Chorus

Oh I believe there are angels among us,

Sent down to us from somewhere up above.

They come to you and me in our darkest hours

To show us how to live, to teach us how to give,

To guide us with a light of love.

When life held troubled times, and had me down on my knees,

There's always been someone there to come along and comfort me.

A kind word from a stranger, to lend a helping hand,

A phone call from a friend, just to say I understand,

And ain't it kind of funny that at the dark end of the road

Someone lights the way with just a single ray of hope.

Chorus

Oh I believe there are angles among us …

They wear so many faces; show up in the strangest places,

To guide us with their mercy, in our time of need.

Chorus

To guide us with the light of love.[6]

There are as many tastes in music as there are our individual personalities. It matters little what your favorite style of music may be, though I recommend that you seek out something comforting and relaxing rather than strong rap music, which may tend to intrude upon a calm mindset. I suggest that you consider the tenderness found within that of classical music such as Bach, Mozart, Pachelbel, Beethoven, or the soothing calmness of the many meditation pieces on the market these days—maybe a waterfall, rain with soothing breezes, or a chant by the Benedictine Monks of Santo Domingo de Silos.

For the young people in our lives that are not yet mature, I recommend a CD by Avalon entitled *The Very Best of Avalon: Testify to Love*. I have discovered that many of our children in this new generation struggle to find their own independence. Having diversified taste in music, their tastes can be refined with little effort from their caregivers by sharing our own taste without criticizing their own choices, knowing their tastes will evolve as they themselves grow and mature.

Throughout this chapter on healing, I have illustrated the survival avenues at our disposal. I can not empathize enough that we first need to address this road less traveled within that of conventional medicine and faith; then and only then can we afford the luxury of seeking out and discovering the many resources that can be found within a large array personal choices at our disposal.

The Healing Powers of Forgiveness

I ask that all who have found themselves on this road less traveled to seek the comfort we so desperately require wherever they may find it, knowing that after the storm will come the calm mind, body, and soul.

As we navigate, we find ourselves challenged within the dissection of emotions that prove to be filled with the sadness of our loss. Forgiveness may not come as easily for some as it may for others. Everything we have discussed thus far reminds us that along with our newfound set of priorities, we will recognize that upon our long road to healing we will be met with obstacles along our way that may seem impossible. Until we reach that point in our personal lives, we may become aware of some of the duties that once were dismissed within the subconscious mind and that may come to us as something neglected or ignored. Remember that each and every one of us is on our personal timetable, filled with the many emotions that will in time, and with effort, slowly become somewhat more manageable to one degree or another.

It is within this normal stage of our personal progress and healthy dissection of our emotions that some will discover the power of forgiveness, if not for ourselves than for another. All of us are aware that with each loss of a child will come the many different sets of circumstances that are attributed to such a loss. Some of our children may have been lost at the hands of others, mindful friends, or complete strangers who have acted without premeditation or malicious intent. As survivors we need to recognize these possibilities as we begin to leave our denial, anger, and guilt behind, becoming aware that in many cases there will be others who may suffer needlessly.

Let me convey to you that I understand that there are some survivors out there who may find this subject incomprehensible and unattainable at best. Know that as we walk this unwelcome fork on our path to a healthier self, the act of forgiveness can at times be met with inner conflict. Some may feel that the act of forgiveness is in some way an act of betrayal to our lost children, while others simply choose not to consider forgiveness due to the interpersonal struggle found within their own turmoil. Please understand, my dear friends, that I remain to, and will forever, empathize with your pain. It is with understanding and kindness that I have brought this subject to your attention, if not for the immediate future then hopefully forgiveness will come to you personally along your personal travels, which all parents, siblings, family members, and close friends will share with total and complete understanding.

We may discover that some family members, friends, co-workers, or complete strangers may have collectively or individually contributed to our loss, even in the smallest of ways, and that those who have accepted responsibility will benefit by the generous gift of forgiveness.

Healing

As I have in the past, within this book I ask that you consider my own personal perspective and thoughts to better help you understand what I have been attempting to relate this far.

Let me ask that for any of us, if we had it within our power to change the direction, the course of someone's life in a positive manner, enabling another to proceed along their path of life with our best wishes, and that they lead a productive, healthy life to the best of their ability, free of the consuming emotion of guilt—would we, should we, could we ignore the opportunity?

It pains me greatly to write and face the undeniable fact that nothing will bring our cherished loved ones back to us. Not in this lifetime. But as we search our hearts and souls and recognize that we have the power for forgiveness and the unselfish empathy to consider these others, knowing that the wonderful power of forgiveness may change the course of their lives as well as creating a snowball effect for generations to come, we will then at some point place that call or write the letter that may, in the smallest of ways, help these others to heal in much the same way we now strive to recover through self-realization. Just as I choose to forgive back in 1978, I accepted the responsibility again recently with the loss of my youngest. I have to admit that for me personally I found little comfort along my travels, but I share with you now that as I hung up the phone, a sense of acceptance came upon me as I pictured my son, recently lost, looking down upon me, his father, with his wonderful smile, and somehow I know he was pleased.

I ask that God be with you along this path, step by step, to be your personal guide to becoming a healthier individual that will be found in self-realization. I believe it's what God wants. Know that God does not want His children to suffer needlessly. Just ask Him.

CONCLUSION

First and foremost I wish to convey to all my dear readers that I am aware that this road we have traveled together hand in hand has at times been difficult as you have faced the many different stages of grief filled with the emotions that may have encumbered your progress to one degree or another. As I have mentioned at the introduction, it remains my strong intention to reach out to you in an up close and personal way by examining what you have already learned after the loss of your child or sibling. We have entered into the area of dissection, whereby we have made it possible to sort our complicated basket of emotions, allowing us to progressively walk upon this path with its many twist and turns.

Just as we have sequentially traveled from chapter to chapter, we have also encountered the many forks on our path that lead us to choose one direction or another. The personal decisions we make will determine our own progression as we will eventually reach the ultimate goal of self-realization as a healthier individual, mentally, physically, and spiritually. It has been and will continue to be the desire of all to remember our lost one and to hold them close to our hearts. This can be a lifetime of joyful memories for you as well as your other family members, knowing you cannot elude the triggers that will enter your state of awareness when you least expect it and bring the tears of a helpless parent, brother, or sister. We will continue to miss our loved one in the physical, knowing they will forevermore be with us in spirit. In our due time we will be reunited in a place with our children, who will patiently wait for us—a place without pain and sorrow, free from illness and discomfort. In this place, we have been told all will be reveled to us that we once could only imagine without comprehension. For those of us in faith, this road less traveled will become less burdensome with time, knowing that there is a promise in which we can hold our trust, believing that our God and Lord will provide the tools needed to guide our lives and show us how to live as well as teach us how to give.

As mentioned, this book was written for the parents and siblings struggling to survive with a healthy mindset after the loss of our children. I hope and pray that as you have traveled from chapter to chapter, you have recognized and become more aware of the many emotions and obstacles that can inhibit healing. You will be called upon by many family members and friends asking for the answers as they too will seek and strive for some type of understanding. They will come to you for comfort, for that magic tool that will provide them with some kind of realization of the tragedy that has touched all who knew and miss our child. As you come to this conclusion, you should have picked up some tools that will enable you to help these others on their own road. Remind them that life is a gift from God and comes with the promise that sometime in the future we will evolve into a healthier self with some reasonable understanding.

When I began writing this book I was aware that if it were to be written, it must be done honestly and unencumbered by many influences, keeping my own emotions in check and acknowledging that just about anything that has ever been written is to some degree influenced by the conscious and subconscious mind. The same holds true for me and mine. I readily accepted this challenge knowing that if this book was to be received as I intended, it must be written in a fashion that would touch so many others reaching for understanding in a personal way only a parent who has lost a child could relate to through experience—one who has traveled upon this lifelong journey picking up the pieces and tools along the way.

This book has been written to you and for you, and by so doing I found that I had to relate to my first loss many years ago back in 1978 rather than reflect upon the most recent loss of my youngest. I had entered into a mindset of years past and the interpersonal development through acute grief then came back to being a productive individual as I entered the healing phase. During the construction stage of this book, I created an illusion that as you read I would find myself standing behind you, unnoticed, with a hand resting upon your shoulder guiding you chapter by chapter in sequence from the worst of times to healing. I am aware that some of what you have read was painful, rekindling memories past; I feel that this is necessary for those who have left the delicate processes of dissection unattended. Remembering that we cannot know where we are going unless we know where we've been, this can be a painful experience without the help of others to walk that path with you. Again, this is why this book has been written. Some friends have said I write as a form of self-therapy; to them I have said, "Of course there is a self-therapeutic value involved here and it cannot be denied or ignored." I've told them, how can it not be? For I too am a parent who cannot elude the rekindling of emotions past as well as present.

For those of you who have yet to make the correlation in my writing, one of the children mentioned in some of the stories shared is my youngest son, Corey, who has yet to be acknowledged in a proper format. This will be rectified soon. Each and every parent, sibling, family member, and loving friend will hold joyful memories of our children lost. Just about everyone will welcome conversations of our children, and almost all will provide the same sentiment: that our child was wonderful, kind, caring, loving, and a joy. Without knowing your child lost, I, like all of you, will easily make a strong correlation to my own children, whether your child was lost as an infant, early childhood, an adolescent, or an adult—it will always be the same. The circumstances that surround our loss will be different, some lost due to tragedy such as suicide, murder, war, terrorist acts, or illness, just to mention a few, regardless of age; one, twenty-one, or sixty-one, they shall always remain our children.

A normal and well-excepted reality within our societies worldwide acceptance of the fact that we as parents are expected to succumb in old age, leaving our children knowing that their day will come upon them as well. They too will leave this world in the physical, with children who will survive. And so it goes in the normal scheme of things, recognizing that heaven is that place for the gray and old. For the minority of us left to survive our children, the physiological effects of emotions in the beginning will seem to be a lifelong struggle. Then as the months and years pass, tragedy will take a backseat to the joy and pride our child left behind, forever embedded in our minds, hearts, and souls.

On my wife's end table in our living room you'll find a small piece of silk with a small butterfly on the right corner that reminds her daily that life is not lost. It reads, "Life is changed, not taken away." Let this serve as a reminder for you as well. Just as the caterpillar cocoons and the stage of metamorphosis begins, so it is with the promise of a miracle from God that what is to emerge is that beautiful butterfly, which will flap its tiny wings and soar effortlessly in the sky above with magnificent wonder. So it is too for our children.

It is my personal wish that you end this book with the memories of your child you hold most dear. You will find four blank pages for you to share your story, giving recognition to your child as an acknowledgment for all to understand the many gifts left behind that you will cherish all the days of your life. Just as all the stories shared by others were given to you with emotion for the sole purpose of reaching out in some small way to help others along their road, so too will you receive the satisfaction of taking pen in hand.

Within the chapter on healing we learned of the several avenues available at our request to fulfill our personal needs as we strive to understand and recognize skills that will at some time in the future lead each and every one of us to a healthier mindset. We now know the day will come when we will again return to the real self, free of acute grief and the turmoil that affects not just ourselves but the lives of our loved ones as well. Of the many tools discovered in the chapter on healing, the benefit of music will touch our hearts as well as our very souls, such as with a song sung by Rod Stewart, "Faith of the Heart":

It's been a long road getting from there to here.
It's been a long time, but my time is finally here,
And I can see my dreams come alive at night; I can touch the sky,
And they're not gonna hold me down no more, no they're not
    gonna change my mind.
'Cause I've got faith of the heart.
I'm going where my heart will take me.
I've got faith to believe I can do anything.
I've got strength of the soul.
No one's going to bend or break me.
I can reach any star; I've got faith, faith of the heart.
It's been a long night trying to find my way.
Been through the darkness, now I finally have my day.
And I will see my dream come alive at last; I will touch the sky,
And they're not gonna hold me down no more.
No they're not gonna change my mind, 'cause I've got faith of the
    heart.

I'm going where my heart will take me; I've got faith to believe I can do anything.

I've got strength of the soul; no one's going to bend or break me. I can reach any star.

I've got faith, faith of the heart.

I know the wind's so cold; I've seen the darkest days,

But now the winds I feel are only winds of change.

I've been through the fire, and I've been through the rain, but I'll be fine.

'Cause I've got faith of the heart. I'm going where my heart will take me.

I've got faith to believe I can do anything.

I've got strength of the soul; no one going to bend or break me.

I can reach any star. I've got faith, I've got faith, faith of the heart.

It's been a long road.[7]

For Our Son
CURTIS JAMES SNYDER
July 12, 1978

At 5:21 a.m. you came into this world with elation shared by your parents as well as the several loving family members waiting with anticipation to hold you, embrace you, and hold your little fingers in their hands with a gentle kiss of welcome. You, as all newborns, arrived with the unmistakable scent of innocence, free from sin, with a parent's strong desire to cultivate and observe the joy of nurturing throughout your lifespan as our children develop their individual personalities.

I remember myself standing, looking upon you, this tiny child separated by a single pane of glass. The minutes passed and seemed like hours, the hours passed and seemed like days. Knowing your time was near, I prayed to God that he take away any pain and discomfort that might be within you. A short time later, as I gazed upon you, your uncontrollable tremors began to subside, your tiny body began to calm, and then as I watched, my prayers were answered as God sent his angel of mercy to cradle you home.

You have never been forgotten. Your mother and I still count the years until our time brings us to you, you who patiently await your mom and dad.

It is not the will of your Father which is in heaven,
that one of these little ones should perish.

Matthew 18:14

Second Acknowledgment

A Letter to My Son, Corey

December 4, 2004

Dear Corey,

This letter will be like no other I have written to you in the past. It is, in fact, my last letter to you, my dear son, and somehow I know you understand.

Twenty-two days after your twenty-fourth birthday this past March, you left us in the physical to go to that place of great reward. Within a blink of an eye, you found yourself in the presence of our Father in a place known as heaven. There you were welcomed and embraced within the light of our loving God. I have to believe that just as our Lord and God patiently awaited your arrival, so will you patiently await the time when all of us will be reunited in that place that no longer eludes you, with the true understanding that those of us who remain on earth simply cannot comprehend with any real understanding. You now reap the rewards of your faith and good works with true happiness, free of the emotions that once found you on earth. I know that you are without sadness, pain, or discomfort. These feelings found within human emotions left you at that very moment your angel carried you from us and into the loving arms of God. You are now reunited with those who preceded you; you have been introduced to your brother Curtis. I can see the two of you playing, with wonderful smiles, running together, experiencing true joy and happiness. I long to be with both of you so much, but I know I must wait for my time when I can once more hold you, kiss you, stroke your hair, and gaze into your eyes with fulfillment and understanding. I imagine us playing and running together in the light of God.

Just as your mother and your older brother miss you so desperately, so do I. We love you so very much. This pain we now feel would be intolerable without the wonderful memories that remain within our hearts and minds that you gave so willingly, free of selfishness. Your mother tells me that as she takes her walks in solitude, she feels your presence in the air, the gentle breezes, and the warmth of the sun that lingers in the sky above. Your brother tells me he too feels your presence with him at every moment, especially at your roadside memorial that he so tenderly maintains. Brian tells me it's a special place where he can go, a place where he can freely speak with you, confide in you still. He has told me that there have been times while at the site that your presence has approached him in a most profound way. He has been overcome knowing it is you who is sitting next to him, at times consoling him, while at other times you still joke with him, enjoying the time filled with his memories with you. I told Brian to cherish these moments and to recognize them as blessings that have come to him from heaven above and not from within the subconscious mind. Your lost brother is with you still and he always will be.

For me, Corey, I find you in prayer, where I can still talk to you, knowing you're okay, knowing you're so happy. I have to. Without it I think I would go insane. You come to me within my uncontrollable despair, filled with the tears that take me from one place in time to another. I know now not to take the wonderful blessings like you for granted. I can look into the eyes of your mother and brother and see you there. I have never lied to you, Corey, and I won't start now. I know my life has forever changed. I know as well that I will recover to some degree, but I have to admit that at this time, as I write you, am not without this hovering cloud that plagues me with emptiness in this world without you. I miss the days past when at your every exit and entrance you came to me smiling, with your warm embrace and that soft kiss that filled my heart and soul with such pride. You never felt embarrassed from early childhood into your early adulthood. It seemed you never forgot what Mom and I always told you and your brother, that no matter how old you got, it made no difference in the presence of whomever, the ties that we shared would never be broken.

What wonderful gifts you and your brother have given Mom and me. Only here can the clouds break, only here can I find hope knowing that if I should die at this very moment, my life has had meaning. I have known the love as a faithful husband. I have had the sheer pleasure in the true form of a gift that you, your brother, and mother have given this undeserving soul. Corey, I can't tell you why God has blessed me in these ways, as well as so many other ways throughout my life, but he did. You, your brother, and your mother are the proof of it.

Thank you, my son, for the inspiration as well as your guidance in our joined effort to help the so many others out there who have their work ahead of them after their own personal loss, a loss like no other. Throughout the manuscript, I have felt your presence at my side, guiding me with a free mind unencumbered by the emotions of the day. Thank you for the person you are, a kind, wonderful humanitarian that chose to console rather then be consoled. You share this quality with your brother Brian. Both of you have received this gift from God.

I could go on forever thanking you, Corey, but am only human and I tire easily. I wish that everyone could have known you the way I do, and still, somewhere within this time and place that all of God's children share, I can't help but feel that they do. Maybe they can make the relationship within the eyes of their own or within the unselfish kindness of others much like yours.

I remember telling you that each and every one of us will encounter others within our lives and that we should be so careful not to prejudge these others. We need to recognize that just about anything we say or do will have some impact. I asked you to be kind and aware of the fact that every life on earth will have some impact upon all we encounter. I told you that our lives here on earth, the things we do and say, will hold a significant value to one degree or another, and that the snowball effect for generations that will follow can be influenced by our actions or the lack thereof and our concern for those we come in contact with in so many different ways.

I cannot speak of you in the past tense. I know we will be together again; I know your life has not ended; I know your life has only changed. I miss you so, I love you so, I hope you receive this letter without worry, without regrets, and I will try my best to do the same.

Thank you, my loving son. Forever yours,
Dad

A Letter From Your Mother

Corey,

How long the days seem without you here. You were my partner in crime, and we had so much fun together. When you, Brian, and I went anywhere together I always knew it would be a day filled with laughter. Most of the laughter has gone out of my life now. When you left all of us here on earth, you took with you a big chunk of our hearts. Now I long for your hugs and kisses on my cheek.

When I walk around the neighborhood, I feel your breath in the wind and your kisses in the sun. I know you will always be with me and I with you. I recall so vividly the time you were here, from birth to end. It seems to have passed in a flash. There isn't a day goes by that you are not on my mind. I constantly recall all of those special times the two of us had. I picture you walking in the door when I was working and remember how proud I was of you. I still wait for you to walk in the door at home. I have been so protective of my kids and would go to bat for all of you at the drop of a hat, and since your accident I find myself wondering if I could have done something different that would have saved you from this horrible end. Please forgive me for all of my mistakes as a mother and know that I did everything I did because I love you. I will let you go now but I will never say good-bye, for I know we will be together someday and I will feel your hugs and your kisses on my cheek once again. I love you and miss you with all my heart, Corey, so wait for me, because I know that I will be with you again.

Love forever,

    Mom

In loving memory of my son

COREY LEE SNYDER

to whom this book is dedicated

March 1980–March 2004

Helpful Resources

The following is a list of some support organizations at your disposal. Not mentioned below is your local place of worship.

DEATH of a CHILD

Compassionate Friends (nationwide)
P.O. Box 3696
Oak Brook, IL 60522-3696
(630) 990-0010
Toll Free (877) 969-0010

AMERICAN SUDDEN INFANT DEATH SYNDROME INSTITUTE (SIDS)
Counseling and Research
509 Augusta Drive
Marietta, GA 30067
(800) 821-6819

DEATH of a CHILD by DRUNK DRIVING
Mothers Against Drunk Driving (MADD)
511 E. John Carpenter Freeway, Suite 700
Irving, TX 75062
(800) 438-6233
Fax (972) 869-2206

SUICIDE

American Association of Suicidology

4201 Connect Ave. NW, Suite 408

Washington, DC 20008

(202) 237-2280

<*http://www.suicidology.org*>

MURDER

Parents of Murdered Children

100 E. 8th St., Room B41

Cincinnati, OH 45202

(513) 721-5683

Toll Free (888) 818-7662

The Compassionate Friends Credo

We need not walk alone.

We are the Compassionate Friends.

We reach out to each with love, with and from understanding and with hope.

Our Children have died at all ages and from many different causes,

But our love for our Children unites us.

Your pain becomes my pain just as your hope becomes my hope.

We come together from all walks of life, from many different circumstances.

We are a unique family because we represent many races and creeds.

We are young, and we are old.

Some of us are far along in our grief, but others still feel a grief so fresh and

So intensely painful that we feel helpless and see no hope.

Some of us have found our faith to be a strong source of strength.

Some of us are angry, filled with guilt or in deep *depression.*

Others radiate an inner peace.

But whatever pain we bring to this gathering of the Compassionate Friends,

It is pain we will share with each other,

Our love for our Children.

We are all seeking and struggling to build a future for ourselves,

But we are committed to building a future together

As we reach out to each other in love

And share the pain as well as the joy,

Share the anger as well as the peace,

Share the faith as well as the doubts,

And help each other to grieve as well as to grow.

WE NEED NOT WALK ALONE.

WE ARE THE COMPASSIONATE FRIENDS.

Recommended Reading

Albom, Mitch. *The Five People You Meet in Heaven.* New York: Hyperion, 2003.

Bennett, William J. *The Book of Virtues*, 1993.

DeStefano, Anthony. *A Travel Guide to Heaven*, 2003.

Eadie, Betty J. *Embraced by the Light*, 1992-1994.

Editors of *Guideposts*. "Angels in Our Midst," 1993.

John Paul II, His Holiness the Pope. *Crossing the Threshold of Hope*, 1994.

Kushner, Harold S. *When Bad Things Happen to Good People.* New York: Avon, 1984.

———. *Living a Life That Matters*, 2001-2002.

Lucado, Max. *The Applause of Heaven*, 1999.

Tatem, Mary. *The Quilt of Life*, 1994.

Yancey, Philip. *Disappointment With God*, 1988.

Sources Cited

1. Douglas Coupland, *Generation X: Tales for an Accelerated Culture* (New York: St. Martin's Griffin, 1991).

2. John Rush, M.D., *Quick Inventory of Depression*, 2001.

3. United States of America Census Bureau, updated 2001

4. World Health-Depression-Emotions, Health Disorders E-Mail; **www.Health** Disorders-Depression.com

5. Don Campbell, *The Mozart Effect*, 1997

6. Alabama, "Angels Among Us," written by Becky Hobbs.

7. Rod Stewart, "Faith of the Heart," written by Diane Warren, 1998.

Printed in the United States
86449LV00004B/154/A